"I believe this is a very timely and
This book is a gift to Black women everywhere.
Jacqueline Horbrook, founder and CEO of Black Christian Influencers

"Natasha Smith's book is a much-needed welcome home to those who have joined the mass exodus of Black women leaving the church in search of other forms of comfort. It is through her words that we remember our Savior sees and cares for us through the grief we carry. May we all remember a day is coming when our Lord will wipe away our tears for good."
Liv Dooley, Bible teacher and podcast host of *The Best Kept Secret with Liv Dooley*

"Natasha Smith's voice is safe, prophetic, and deeply necessary. With gravitas and love, *Black Woman Grief* honors the depths of pain that Black women carry and the collective experience of suffering, while moving the reader toward unapologetic kingdom hope and healing."
Aubrey G. Sampson, pastor, podcaster, and author of *The Louder Song*

"In *Black Woman Grief*, Natasha Smith provides a safe place for Black women to address what's grieving us while taking us by the hand and gently paving a path toward wholeness. Through biblical wisdom, healthy practical examples, and her personal lived experiences with grief, Natasha reframes the idea of the strong Black woman, provides language for our pain, and gives every woman who feels like she's drowning in grief a lifeline of hope. This book is a gift to the Black woman's soul and is more necessary than ever."
Christina Patterson, founder and president of Beloved Women

"With deep compassion, Natasha Smith gives voice to the grief and trauma Black women carry, providing a path for lament and healing. This book is a vital resource for anyone looking to honor those emotions while finding hope in the process."
Lorenzo A. Watson, president and CEO of the Christian Community Development Association

BLACK WOMAN

A GUIDE TO HOPE AND WHOLENESS

GRIEF

NATASHA SMITH

FOREWORD BY QUANTRILLA ARD

ivp

An imprint of InterVarsity Press
Downers Grove, Illinois

InterVarsity Press
P.O. Box 1400 | Downers Grove, IL 60515-1426
ivpress.com | email@ivpress.com

InterVarsity Press® is the publishing division of InterVarsity Christian Fellowship/USA®. For more information, visit intervarsity.org.

All Scripture quotations, unless otherwise indicated, are taken from The Holy Bible, New International Version®, NIV®. Copyright © 1973, 1978, 1984, 2011 by Biblica, Inc.™ Used by permission of Zondervan. All rights reserved worldwide. www.zondervan.com. The "NIV" and "New International Version" are trademarks registered in the United States Patent and Trademark Office by Biblica, Inc.™

While any stories in this book are true, some names and identifying information may have been changed to protect the privacy of individuals.

Published in association with the Mary DeMuth Literary, https://marydemuthliterary.com.

"Feelings Wheel" figure adapted from "The Feelings Wheel" in Gloria Wilcox, *Feelings: Converting Negatives to Positives* (Kearney, NE: Morris Publishing, 2001).

The publisher cannot verify the accuracy or functionality of website URLs used in this book beyond the date of publication.

Cover design: David Fassett
Interior design: Daniel van Loon
Images: Getty Images Plus: ©Terry Vine / DigitalVision; Getty Images: ©J_art / Moment, ©oxygen / Moment

ISBN 978-1-5140-0964-2 (print) | ISBN 978-1-5140-0965-9 (digital)

Printed in the United States of America ∞

Library of Congress Cataloging-in-Publication Data
A catalog record for this book is available from the Library of Congress.

31 30 29 28 27 26 25 | 12 11 10 9 8 7 6 5 4 3 2 1

TO ALL BLACK WOMEN.

This book is dedicated to you— the beautiful, the resilient,

the powerful, the nurturing, the bold. You are the

heartbeat of communities, the keepers of wisdom, and

the embodiment of grace. Your courage and brilliance

light the way for future generations. May you find the

hope, healing, and wholeness you deserve.

God is within you; you will not fail.

CONTENTS

FOREWORD

QUANTRILLA ARD, PHD

HELLO.

I'm a Black Woman.

I am a griever.

I have Black Woman Grief.

Grief knocks loudly at our doors, unexpectedly. It weaves its way into our lives unannounced. For Black women, however, grief is not a stranger. It is and has been a common part of our existence. I confess that it has been like a program running in the background of my life for so long that I can't remember the very first time it appeared. Sometimes grief is like that.

We often name our grief and share our grief stories by the largeness of the experience, yet dismiss the smaller, less noticeable ways that grief journeys alongside us. Black women know grief from the time we are conceived in our mothers' wombs, and yet we persist. Many of us carry Black woman grief forward like an embedded chromosome in our DNA. Contrary to popular belief, what doesn't kill us *doesn't* make us stronger.

Black women need resources and strategies that help us name our grief, sit with it, and carve out a path outlined with hope.

Natasha Smith is a gift. Her words in this book are too. Living as a griever can feel lonely, and being called to give hope and encouragement and to inspire other grievers can feel scary. Sharing our stories bonds us not only in our collective grief but also specifically in our shared Black woman grief. Community is one of the greatest helps in grief. The desire to hide our grief in a world that makes us feel "othered" is normal—however, we are not meant to go on this journey alone. We need each other. What Natasha shares in the following pages is a life raft for Black women who may feel stuck in their grief.

With that said, Black woman, let's chat.

This, sister, is your resource, a necessary guide to lean into when you have lived without the vocabulary for and context of your grief for so long. If like me, you find yourself haphazardly falling down the rabbit hole of the superwoman schema[1]—a mental health syndrome where Black or African American women feel that they must suppress their emotions, dependence, and vulnerability, and put caregiving ahead of their own self-care all while presenting a strong front—you are in the right place.

When I think of the grief that I carry as I write this foreword, I think of the current communal grief Black women all over the world are navigating. One of those is the assassination of Sonya Massey, an American Black woman, at the hands of those employed by the system she reached out to for protection and safety. In this book, you will notice recurring themes of anticipatory and compounded grief. As the manuscript for this book was being developed, there were grievances Black women were carrying, and as Natasha so aptly describes in chapter five, "This event will already exist in the shadow of many others like it." And just like that, by the time you read this foreword, unfortunately, Sonya Massey's story will be a shadow. Black woman grief.

I have a few questions for you to ponder as you prepare to read. When was the last time you gave yourself permission to hold your grief, Black woman? When was the last time you stopped to admit that pain was present? When did you last feel the power of community holding you up? Are you ready to face your Black woman grief with tools and encouragement to support a hope-filled life?

Black woman, in these pages, you will see yourself at the intersection of your various identities grieving the loss of what was, what is, and what could have been. You will also find the strength and courage to believe that your grief does not preclude your joy.

A brief note for those who are not Black women: this book is a love letter to Black women who grieve and a road map for those who know and love Black women who grieve. In these pages, you will see someone you care for. Educate yourself by exploring the phenomenon that is Black woman grief. Please do not ignore the draw to not only acknowledge grief through the lens of Black women but also to see our grief in all its harrowing glory. If you are asking yourself if "Black Woman Grief" is a thing, it is. If you are asking yourself, "Why does grief have to be described in this way? Grief has no color," this book is for you also. Natasha craftily weaves together encouragement from everyday examples, biblical themes, and personal narratives from her own life to bring the reader into the world of Black woman grief—a world that is often overlooked, dismissed, and undervalued. You will be challenged to not look away and to hold space for Black woman grief and its generational impact.

Black woman, I can't wait for you to turn the page. You will be encouraged and helped in these chapters in a special way by someone who can relate to you and who is navigating her own Black woman grief. My hope for you as you read is that you will feel the very present hands of God holding you and comforting you in your Black woman grief.

INTRODUCTION

Momma! Momma!

GEORGE FLOYD

Dehumanized.

Targeted.

Hated.

Hunted.

Murdered.

Brutally shot and killed.

These words have dominated headlines about our Black brothers and sisters over the past several years.

But every Black woman in America took special notice when forty-six-year-old George Floyd called "Momma! Momma!" in his last moments of life.

He lay chest down, cheek against the pavement, as an officer held a knee against George's neck for over nine minutes—even as Floyd continuously told him he couldn't breathe. With two other cops restraining him and another preventing people from intervening, Floyd died in front of bystanders that day. It was all caught on video.

Floyd's mother had been dead for two years when he called for her. It makes his death more painful. It turns our attention to how he remembered his mom, a Black woman, during a moment of deep distress. As he was taking his last breaths, he pointed us to the one who gave him life.

For Black women, it doesn't have to be our child for us to feel like it's our child. We often grow up in villages. Aunties and uncles are like moms and dads. Our cousins are like brothers and sisters. Our neighbors are like blood relatives. So when one hurts, we all hurt. Our history, our culture, and our story weave us together in such a way that we grieve in community.

My nieces and nephews grew up in the same household with me and my parents, who helped raise them. My nephew George calls me Big Sis. This is similar for many Black women who claim their nieces, nephews, and cousins as their own. My mom went a step further and loved all the children in the neighborhood. She would talk to them the way she talked to us, giving them unwanted advice and telling them about Jesus whether they wanted to hear it or not. In the same breath she would ask, "How's your family doing? Do you know Jesus?" They knew my mom loved them, and she still does.

WE ARE NOT ALONE

We are all interconnected. And Black women are at the center of it all. We have the biggest hearts.

My sister Sharon was so exemplary of this. As a cafeteria manager and bus driver, she knew all the kids in her school. Walking around town with her, I often heard "Hey, Ms. Sharon" from kids passing by. She would grin the way she always did because those kids were a part of her. As a Black woman, it's almost innate to love so *big* and *wide* with all we've got. Because maybe we feel that love is the biggest thing we have. We know love never fails.

Because of our village mentality as Black women, witnessing deaths due to unjust police brutality ignites grief among us. It feels as if we're drowning while everyone else is watching or going about daily life unbothered by the horrific scene happening in front of them. It's silenced grief, rarely seen by passersby. But from Black woman to Black woman, we know.

It leaves us with a rallying cry: "We can't breathe."

A story becomes a high-profile case, and then when it's over, everything goes dark. Again. Grief settles in more deeply because the world continues to turn while our world is at a standstill—even though at any moment it could come unhinged. And what we wish could be normal conversations at home become conversations we *must* have with our kids and in our Black communities.

"Straighten your clothes."

"Put on a belt."

"Stand up straight."

"Keep your hands out of your pockets."

"Hold your head up."

"Don't wear that hood on your head."

"Keep calm. Stay polite."

We live in a world where having these conversations is necessary for us to live.

Black women most often experience grief in one of several ways: the early loss of a parent, the early loss of a spouse, the early loss of a sibling, and/or the death of a child.[1] While these are personal losses, we also experience living losses such as racism or career limitations due to discrimination, poverty, identity, time, and opportunities.

YOU ARE NOT ALONE

For context, *Black* and *African American* are used interchangeably in the text. The conversations within this book focus on the Black woman's experience within the United States. Also, I use the terms *grief*, *mourning*, and *bereavement* in the following ways:

- *Grief* is a normal yet complex and innate human experience that stems from an undesirable event, affecting not only our mental and physical well-being but also our spirit and overall quality of life.[2]
- *Mourning* is an outward expression of that grief, including cultural and religious customs surrounding the death. It is also the process of adapting to life after loss.[3]
- *Bereavement* is a period of grief and mourning after a loss.[4]

My prayer is that this book will make space for the grief that comes with being a Black woman in America. I pray this book will provide you the opportunity to grieve, lament, and honor the losses and traumas you have experienced. I pray this book will bring hope and healing.

Dear Black woman, you are not alone in feeling alone. You are not alone in wondering about the what ifs. You are not alone in grieving alongside every Black woman who has lost her child due to racial violence and injustice. You are not alone in feeling as if no one cares, as if things in our country and our world will never change, as if all hope is lost.

We think we can't overcome our worst moments, but Jesus is the One who overcame the world and gives us hope that we can overcome too—that one day all hatred will be overcome with love. And we don't have to wait for heaven to experience the life God intended for us. God wants us to live well *now*, even in this grief-filled world.

So how does God tend to our hearts, and how does he hold us during these times of grief?

What does it mean to be kept by God and to hold our peace?

How can we overcome and redeem the moments that feel like another sad story on repeat?

How do we recognize and deal with this grief?

How do we heal and stir our faith in the hope of Christ?

How do we live well amidst the grief we encounter as Black women?

If you've desperately needed the answers to these questions, you're in the right place. Keep reading, as this book will give you space to grieve and just breathe, dear Black woman.

1

STRONG BLACK WOMAN

Come to me, all you who are weary and
burdened, and I will give you rest.

MATTHEW 11:28

"YOU'RE ONE OF THE STRONGEST PEOPLE I KNOW."
These words from my friend were like nails screeching on a
chalkboard. Though the sentiment was endearing, I knew it to
be untrue. Yet I get this often. In these moments, my heart stops
for a minute and I think, *You give me too much credit.*

Those words seem equivalent to "If I were you, I would've
lost my mind."

But under varying circumstances, we truly don't know what
we'll do until we do it. We have an innate ability to endure
things we never thought we could. Sometimes simply surviving
is a feat of its own. Remember Oprah Winfrey's famed line in
The Color Purple: "All my life I had to fight."

At times, that *is* what life feels like as a Black woman: a fight.
Wrestling over how to make life better for ourselves and our

loved ones without losing ourselves in the process. Battling for equality in the workplace and in our homes. Fighting for all these things while trying to not look like the angry Black woman. Malcolm X said, "The most disrespected person in America is the black woman. The most unprotected person in America is the black woman. The most neglected person in America is the black woman."[1]

We must fight stereotypes. Not all of us come from broken homes, and not all Black women are single parents. Yet, for those of us who are single parents, not all of us struggle in the ways some people think.

As Black women, we fight against European beauty standards: our hair, our melanin, and our bodies. We are beautiful, yet when we're compared to others, we're told we aren't enough.

So we find ourselves constantly fighting.

We fight for our relationships, for our well-being, for our loved ones, for our friendships, for our sanity, and simply for ourselves.

We fight.

Then we fight some more.

And as Black women, we are tired.

So when my friend told me, "You're so strong," I felt anything but strong. I was beyond tired.

I'd just shared with her how the year so far had been excruciatingly hard as it related to grief. Bandages were ripped off old wounds and sealed places of my heart were opened, exposed to the elements for the sake of attempting to heal. All because healing begins when we name the thing that has hurt us. And even as I write this, more grief is to come later in the year—my late sister Sharon's birthday will be on November 13, the anniversary of my sister Angie's death will fall on November 22, followed by Thanksgiving days later, and then Christmas. It happens every year.

There's no escaping the grief, it seems.

Yet, it's the things we leave unsaid that we battle the most. For so many Black women, grief is the unspoken thing—the invisible pain.

But as the saying goes, "Thank God we don't look like what we've been through." Can I get an amen?

So yes, being strong is a beautiful thing, but it can also be isolating. What is it about appearing strong that makes us feel so empowered? We often hear things like, "Nothing fazes her," "She never cries," "She's not afraid of anything," "Life never gets her down."

I think about my mom and her losses: her miscarriage, and the losses of her dad, two adult children, grandchildren, great-grandchildren, her husband, and several siblings. I think about how she's dealt with them all. On the outside looking in, I admit I've said countless times, "She's the strongest woman I know."

You've probably said this about your mom. And it's probably been said about yourself and other Black women.

Take a moment and pause.

Now, name all the strong women you know.

Chances are that those who come to mind—including Black matriarchs like Harriet Tubman and Rosa Parks—all experienced a hardship, a devastating loss, or some type of suffering. But we often fail to realize the strong Black woman badge is only earned through sacrifice. You may have seen the meme floating around on social media that says, "Check on your strong friend."

We might say, "Check on the strong Black woman."

FAMILIAL EXPECTATIONS AND CAREGIVING

Research suggests that caregiving is a historical and cultural tradition of Black women.[2] And it can easily seem as though Black women are disproportionately caregivers within their homes. There is insurmountable loss because Black women who are caregivers are deemed better at caring for everyone else than themselves. In my own family, the role of caregiver has been predominately taken by women.

Over the years, my mom's caregiving responsibilities have involved raising her children and grandchildren, tending to her husband's health—including his chest problems, stroke, and diabetes—caring for her mother, providing both paid and voluntary caregiving services in the community, volunteering at church, and looking after kids in the neighborhood. My mom would be considered part of the "sandwich generation": individuals who find themselves caring for their aging parents and their children and/or grandchildren.[3]

At the age of eighty, my mom is still helping to care for her one-hundred-year-old mother, which is commendable. We all love that Grandma can live at home and be cared for by family. Yet, I know the deep challenge this has placed on my mom. There were times when she had to choose between supporting us, my dad, or my grandma. And with my mom's impending health issues, continuing to be her mom's caregiver is challenging.

My mom lived with us for three months after being newly diagnosed with diabetes. It was challenging navigating the landscape of this new-to-us disease, understanding how it impacted our daily lives and the new limitations it imposed on my mom's life. This experience reminded me of the times I cared for babies while in the throes of fresh grief; I faced the unknowns of navigating new terrain, balancing self-care and my responsibilities of caring for my children.

We don't need to have kids to be deemed part of the sandwich generation. As the youngest girl in the family, I was on baby-sitter duty for years, especially during the summers. During my tween and teen years, I babysat my nieces and nephews. It was expected of me. I loved it most times (until I felt I deserved to be paid for my labor). Still, babysitting them taught me a lot. And I have great relationships with my nieces and nephews that I may not have had otherwise.

I thought I'd drown from caring for our youngest son, a bouncing baby boy. Since I had my kids later than my older sisters did, my parents were much older at the time. I felt a little salty because I didn't receive the same support my parents gave my sisters—which made it seem as if all the caregiving fell on me. Granted, my dad passed away before really getting to know my youngest kids. And my mom was and is still caring for her mom.

My younger cousin was the primary caregiver to her mom, my aunt, who was diagnosed with stage 4 cancer. Though she has brothers, the caregiving weight was put on her shoulders.

This isn't to say that caring for our loved ones is a burden. However, it takes a toll on our ability to process grief and trauma. We often put self-care on the back burner because we don't even have time to tie our shoes. We constantly do and do and do for others, neglecting ourselves until someone has to do for us.

My grandma had eleven children, and only the women have been part of the caregiving rotation. I'm pretty sure it's not because they're the only ones capable. It's still hard to see my mom in a demanding caregiving role at her age. This confirms to me that Black women remain primary caregivers throughout their lifetimes. How can we rest? How can we balance it all?

Along with our grief, we often carry the losses and the experiences of our family who have gone before us and who are now with us. And this often shapes and informs expectations and coping mechanisms within the family.[4] My mom and so many of us Black women carry so much.

I've seen my mom cry at funerals, and I've heard her crying in the wee hours of the night while praying. I've done the same: tucked the grief away neatly to not make a scene in front of others—even my family. With the immensity of loss experienced, someone on the outside looking in would say, "You're so strong." But we carry these "strong Black woman" labels because no one sees what happens when the mask is lowered in the shower or on the bathroom floor, when we can't see through the tears streaming down our faces. But I understand the importance of letting my kids see me cry. I need to let them know how important it is to process and express emotion. We don't have to hide behind masks, because it's not healthy.

So I pray as you continue to read this book that you feel freedom in expressing your exhaustion, frustrations, hurt, and pain. To help your kids and those around you know it's okay to not be okay.

Now, let it sit for a moment. And just breathe.

Because none of us is ever as strong as we appear to be.

DEFINING STRONG

Being strong is a compliment, right? Strength is valued in our society and culture, particularly in the Black community. It's seen as a badge of honor and respect.

But what does it even mean to be *strong*?

It can mean having the power to lift heavy weights or perform other physically demanding tasks. Or it's being able to withstand great force or pressure. Merriam-Webster defines *strong* as "having or being marked by great physical power, having moral or intellectual power, and having great resources (such as wealth or talent)."[5] Does that sound like you or someone you know? Or does it just sound like a stereotype of Black women?

Research suggests the perception of the physically and psychologically strong Black woman dates to slavery and informs today's perception of Black women as determined, self-controlled, independent individuals. They have a strong work ethic while caregiving and sacrificing their wants and needs to support their family and community.[6] What characteristics come to mind when you think of a Black woman?

I think of resilience. The reality of being strong comes at a cost. Most often, we are strong because we have no other choice. We appear strong because we keep our true feelings and emotions to ourselves so as not to appear weak or without faith. Research suggests there is a high correlation between anxiety and depression among Black women.[7] Yet, the hardships we experience are chalked up to "Well, it's just a part of life." This perspective has been passed down through generations. My teen and young adult years were filled with sayings like, "Don't depend on a man"—yet now it makes me think of times when I'm challenged to depend on Jesus. Maybe this thinking carries over into my spiritual life. And maybe yours as well.

LEARNING TO LEAN ON GOD'S STRENGTH

Growing up, my three sisters and I were encouraged to be self-sufficient and independent. There's nothing wrong with holding your own. But for us, this translated into never asking for help, doing everything ourselves, and believing "if I want it done right, I have to do it myself." It overwhelmed me and, if I'm honest, it continues to do so at times. Have you become overwhelmed by the weight of being strong?

In Black religious culture, talking about our struggles openly is often seen as a sign of weakness, disbelief, or lack of faith. So we put up a front to appear strong. We throw around platitudes when asked "How are you doing?" We know the correct response is, "I'm blessed and highly favored." All the while, we are broken deep down and don't know how we're going to recover. We're stuck in "fake it until you make it" mode. This also keeps us hesitant to seek professional help and instead leads us to push our emotions to the side, to disregard how we feel, and to deal with it alone.

To maintain the façade that we are strong, we may avoid things that keep us from grieving or outwardly expressing our grief. I avoided the collection of documents and pictures of my son I placed into adoptive care over twenty years ago. Spring of 2024, I pulled them down from the attic, gathering pictures and items for a grief art class series I participated in for birth moms. And just as I expected, fresh grief ensued. This is why we avoid things that trigger grief. What have you avoided for the sake of appearing strong?

God's take on being strong is different from ours and the world's because God's strength is made perfect in weakness (2 Corinthians 12:9). We find our hope and strength in God. The apostle Paul wrote, "We have this hope as an anchor for the soul, firm and secure. It enters the inner sanctuary behind the curtain" (Hebrews 6:19). Paul also wrote, "That is why, for Christ's sake, I delight in weaknesses, in insults, in hardships, in persecutions, in difficulties. For when I am weak, then I am strong" (2 Corinthians 12:10).

Simply put, we were not made to be strong. And we were never made to do everything for everybody or be available to everybody at all times. That is God's job. When we think of our very creation, we were made from the rib of Adam, who was made from dust. It is written, "Then the LORD God formed a man from the dust of the ground and breathed into his nostrils the breath of life, and the man became a living being" (Genesis 2:7).

Dust is defined as "fine, dry powder consisting of tiny par-
ticles of earth or waste matter lying on the ground or surfaces
or carried in the air."[8] Have you ever wondered why God chose
dust to form us? Why not stone or wood or iron? I believe this
demonstrates how we were never made to be strong without
him, "for he knows how we are formed, he remembers that we
are dust" (Psalm 103:14). If we can acknowledge our true weaknesses and our need for Jesus, why do we struggle to rely on
him when he is the most reliable One? Sometimes it's because
we encounter people who let us down, so we have no choice
but to act strong. Sometimes we experience something we are
utterly unprepared for, such as the loss of a parent as a child.

You may have heard the saying, "What doesn't kill you makes
you stronger." This adage from the nineteenth-century German
philosopher Friedrich Nietzsche is generally used as an affirmation of resilience.[9] But in the experience of Black women,
what doesn't kill us gives us trauma. We are left with things
we have to work out and work through. Left unresolved, these
things can push us to project our trauma onto others. These
aftereffects may negatively impact our loved ones, coworkers,
and colaborers for the kingdom, and may even ripple beyond
the present to future generations.

Let's stop right here. This is your time to just *be*.

This is your time to peel off layers and layers of the masks
you wear, to be who you are in Christ—his daughter, leaning
and depending on him, looking to the hills where your help
comes from, and knowing your help comes from the Lord
(Psalm 121:1-2). Our confidence and strength lie in the One who

lives in us. When we are strong in our own strength, we have the potential to break. Our mental, spiritual, and physical health suffers. We draw from a finite well of our self-sufficiency instead of the infinite well of living water Jesus wants to provide for us.

The ability to endure grief and suffering seemingly on our own is perceived as a gift by others, but it feels like a curse. I heard this illustration of grief: if we get into a bad traffic accident and have to be in a full body cast as a result, others will recognize the physical pain we are in. But when we have no external indicators of the internal suffering, pain, and grief we are carrying, it appears we are fine.

People see us and wonder, "I don't know how you're still smiling despite what you've been through."

And we say, "It's because of God."

JESUS' INVITATION TO CARRY OUR BURDENS

I think about what we've been through as Black people from slavery to now and everything in between. We are often counted out, with the odds against us because of our race, but we are resilient people. Some things have changed, but so many haven't. It all seems like a heavy burden.

Yet Jesus said, "Come to me, all you who are weary and burdened, and I will give you rest. Take my yoke upon you and learn from me, for I am gentle and humble in heart, and you will find rest for your souls. For my yoke is easy and my burden is light" (Matthew 11:28-30).

A yoke is a farming tool, a wooden crosspiece fastened over the necks of two animals and attached to the plow or cart they pull. Jesus uses this terminology in Matthew to illustrate that when we are yoked with him—connected and partnered with him—we find rest in him. When we are yoked with anything other than him, we are prone to burdens.

What are you yoked with? What burdens are you carrying?

We may find ourselves yoked with wrong ideals and expectations due to our culture, tradition, or religion. But we can break free from these yokes through the power of the Holy Spirit and prayer. We can exchange those yokes for the yoke of God. And we can lean on Jesus even when we feel strong. We need him in every season and every circumstance.

There are very real battles you have faced, are facing, or will face. But the good news is God wants to fight your battles.

When the Israelites marched out of Egypt from slavery, Moses assured them, "The LORD will fight for you; you need only to be still" (Exodus 14:14). Yet when they found themselves being pursued by Pharaoh's army, they immediately blamed Moses: "Didn't we say to you in Egypt, 'Leave us alone; let us serve the Egyptians'? It would have been better for us to serve the Egyptians than to die in the desert!" (Exodus 14:12). They gave up on God even before giving him a chance. Let this not be our story, even in grief. God fights for us, and he is our strength.

Just as God told Joshua to "be strong and courageous," he tells us the same. He also commands us, "Do not be afraid; do not be discouraged, for the LORD your God will be with you wherever you go" (Joshua 1:9).

We attempt to be strong through our abilities, education, skills, and experience. We allow what has happened to us to "make us strong." Yet, this reminds me of how the same boiling water that softens a potato also hardens an egg. What we deem as being strong only hardens our hearts because of what we've endured—so we put up walls, not realizing that we shut out both the bad and the good. Of course, we *should* be encouraged to be strong and courageous, but only through the strength of the Lord.

Let this be your permission to stop putting up the front that you're so strong for the sake of your family, friends, coworkers, boss, and kids. You don't have to pretend anymore.

What was happening in Joshua's life that God had to tell him at least three times to be strong and courageous? There was going to be a big change in power and leadership. Joshua was to pick up the mantle from Moses, one of the most significant patriarchs of our Christian faith. The children of Israel, the same ones who complained during Moses' leadership, were the ones he would be leading.

What's more, it was up to Joshua to lead the people into the Promised Land. And there were giants there! But can you imagine the people's doubt was worse than the giants?

However, God telling Joshua to be strong and courageous was not as important as the words that followed: "For the LORD your God will be with you wherever you go" (Joshua 1:9). God is with us. He lives in us. He is our strength. We no longer have to carry the weight of the world on our shoulders because God carries it for us.

THE FIRST STRONG WOMAN

To close out this chapter about being a strong woman, it's important and necessary to talk about Eve, who was not only the first woman who ever lived but also the first to ever grieve. Made from the rib of Adam, created by the hand of God, she was perfection. Everything she needed was there with her in the Garden of Eden. She didn't carry what we carry today— no shame, no insecurities, no worries, no sickness, no world systems to dismantle, no politics; no tears, no pain, no grief. But sin entered the world through the hands of Eve and then her husband, Adam.

Why would Eve sin when she had everything? The thing is, she didn't know she had everything. While we get to be onlookers reading Genesis from beginning to end, Eve didn't know what was unfolding as she was deceived and manipulated by the serpent. She often gets a bad rap, but she deserves the same grace that has been extended to us.

So yes, Eve listened to the lies of the enemy: "You will not certainly die" (Genesis 3:4). Eve and Adam's sin led to them getting kicked out of Eden, to women experiencing pain in childbearing, and to husbands ruling over their wives. Most importantly, it opened the door for death and grief to enter the earth. Genesis 4 tells of how Eve's two sons, Cain and Abel, offered sacrifices to the Lord. When the Lord favored Abel's sacrifice and not Cain's, an angry Cain killed Abel. Not only had Eve (and Adam) grieved the traumatic loss of being put out of Eden, along with the other consequences, they were now also grieving the death of their son Abel.

In all these variant losses, Eve is the first woman in the Bible to grieve—and the first woman who felt she had to be strong as she grieved the murder of one son while the other son wandered off. Still, amid her suffering, she gives us an example of how to hope and trust in God. Genesis 4:25 reads, "She gave birth to a son and named him Seth, saying, 'God has granted me another child in place of Abel, since Cain killed him.'" Her words affirm the Lord's care for her—and for us.

God sees all and knows all. He knows the desire of your heart. And when it seems as if your prayers have fallen on deaf ears, the Lord hears them still. He is moving and working on your behalf. "For the eyes of the LORD range throughout the earth to strengthen those whose hearts are fully committed to him" (2 Chronicles 16:9).

Dear Black woman,

You've had to be strong for way too long. Now is the time to let the King of glory be your strength—not just sometimes, but all the time. Lay down your strivings, your fighting, your masks, and your feelings of inadequacy at the feet of Jesus.

Yes, you are a strong woman, always carrying the weight of the world on your shoulders, putting others' needs before yours, and tirelessly caring for your loved ones, your neighbors, and your church. Watching over them and praying for them. And maybe even grieving them. I'm lifting you up today.

I pray the love, peace, and strength of God will surround you and you will feel his presence. As you go to him, he will pour into you what you need, and he will fill you up to overflowing where you have emptied. I pray you will rest in God's comfort. In Jesus' name. Amen.

2

WORTHY OF LOVE

She is more precious than rubies; nothing
you desire can compare with her.

PROVERBS 3:15

WE WERE BORN BLACK, and there's no changing that. We didn't get to choose our skin color, eye color, or hair texture. Martin Luther King Jr. dreamed one day we wouldn't be judged by the color of our skin but by the content of our character. We are not there yet.

But I feel we're finally starting to embrace what makes us Black women. We have embraced our beautiful sun-kissed skin and our textured hair, whether wavy, curly, kinky, or coily. The huge wave of naturalistas showed us the beauty of those who choose to wear their natural hair with no constraints. One thing I love is our versatility. We can wear our hair in an Afro one day, then turn around and get braids or faux locs, throw on a wig, or rock some extensions. But we haven't always been here.

Have you heard the phrase "melanin poppin'"? Melanin produces pigments in our skin and gives it that beautiful color, from varying shades of brown to dark as coal. We each have different levels of melanin in our skin based on several factors, including genetics.[1] I used to think my brown skin was gifted to me by kisses from the sun, as if living closer to the equator makes your skin darker. But now I know better. Our beautiful skin comes from *the* Son, our Creator in heaven. When God made you and me, dear Black woman, he said, "It is good." Let's take a moment to pause and say, "God made me. And I am good."

When I think about being comfortable in our skin, I think about those who represent Black women well, whether on the big screen, in music, or in ministry. In *The Woman King*, Viola Davis plays a Black woman warrior who trains and leads a great army of Black women to fight on behalf of their king and their tribe. Because of her invaluable contribution to the protection of the kingdom, Davis's character is influential to the king. She has seen how foreign colonizers have come to trade her people for weapons, and she does not stand for it. She convinces the king to trade other things such as palm oil instead of people. Then she leads the army to fight to show that her people are more valuable than anything the colonizers could trade.

The film, based on historical events, reminds me that we were once Black kings and queens in our homeland. But due to exploitation and the slave trade, among other events, our value decreased so we were seen as less than human. We stood nearly naked on trading blocks, even at the hands of our own people. Beginning centuries ago, we embarked on a continuous journey to understand and embrace our worth.

Yet it seems as if we are still convincing the world that we are worthy of love and respect. That we are worthy of so much *more* than what we have experienced. Today, we allow culture, the media, our environment, and our upbringing to define our worth. What a difference it would make if we were taught our true value from a young age.

LOOKING FOR LOVE

In my teen years, I believed if I could get a boy to look at me or like me, I was doing pretty good. I remember when the approval of boys was one of the greatest barometers of my self-worth. My mom would caution me, "Don't be messing with them boys." But she still didn't convince me otherwise.

I was searching for my worth and measuring it by my popularity. But when we don't know our worth, we allow others to assign it to us—opening the door to others making us feel worthless. In some cases, a lack of self-worth can easily lead girls and women to be taken advantage of by teenage boys with raging hormones ("If you love me, you'll do _____ for me") and even full-grown men. I found this to be true in my life, like the line from the Broadway musical *Hamilton*, "If you stand for nothing, Burr, what'll you fall for?" If you don't stand for something, you'll fall for anything.

Black women experience intimate partner violence at higher rates than women overall, at 40 percent.[2] Having grown up in a family of four Black girls, I've seen my share of unhealthy relationships, from sexual abuse to domestic violence. I have broken up more fights than I can count, sat in emergency rooms wondering what the outcome would be, and visited several jails and courthouses. Being the youngest, it was a lot for me to take in.

I believed going to college would change a lot of things for me. I remember feeling so proud when I headed off to college with a group of my white friends, particularly white males, who I'd shared honors and advanced placement classes with. One of them was even our high school class valedictorian! But one of my proudest moments was seeing each of them on campus and learning they had all dropped out of the engineering program I'd stayed in and would graduate from. This gave me so much satisfaction at the time, because I didn't know where my true worth was from. Rather, my self-worth was clouded by culture and the world. I thought outperforming my white counterparts would make me better somehow. Maybe you have had this thought too or feel this way now. But this should not be the case.

I looked to my education as an indication of self-worth. But my degree didn't make me any less Black, and the search for my worth inevitably started with one thing and led to another. It progressed from dating the cutest guy, to earning the highest grades, to getting into the best school, to being hired for the best job, to making the most money. The list went on and on. In the end, these things do not change who we are. In the end, we still must deal with ourselves and navigate through life as Black women.

Our worth as Black women is often hidden, whether by ourselves or by others. The movie *Hidden Figures* portrays the story of four Black women—Dorothy Vaughan, Katherine Johnson, Mary Jackson, and Christine Darden—who greatly impacted the aerospace engineering field while working at

NASA but were not recognized for their contributions at the time. In 2022, I learned of the "Six Triple Eight," an all-Black women's army corps unit that served during World War II. In March of that year, almost *eighty* years after the war ended, they were recognized with the Congressional Gold Medal for their service.[3] Like, whoa. I'm thankful these Black women are receiving the recognition they deserve, but I also can't help thinking, *Why did it take so long?*

It's grievous to not be recognized for doing something great. But how do we come to truly understand our worth? We must remember that what we have sought after and achieved on earth can be stripped away at any time. It takes biblical truth to know who we are in Christ and who he created us to be.

FINDING WORTH IN CHRIST

Christ found me in my sophomore year of high school during an event at church, where various singing groups and gospel choirs were gathered. I was a member of a district gospel choir in my area. We were a combined choir from different churches, and y'all, we could *sing*. We had practiced for weeks and weeks, even adding in special practices to make sure everything sounded top-notch. That night after we finished our selections, we came back to our section in the congregation to enjoy the remainder of the program and to listen to the other choirs and singing groups. But then it happened.

During what felt like an intermission, the preacher extended an invitation to salvation, an altar call. I'd heard that speech before, but this time something caught my heart. I felt a literal tugging, both a gentle nudge and an urgency to loosen my grip on the pew in front of me.

"Excuse me," I said, as I passed each person sitting in my row.

I made my way to the front of the church. I thought I would feel embarrassed, but I felt like it was just me and Jesus. As if everything I'd heard and learned about him made sense all at once. Not just in my head, but in my heart—what I would come to know as a bearing witness in my spirit of who God is. I felt overwhelmed by a sense of pureness, and richness of God's love for me, that he died for me, and if it was only for me, he still would have done it. Just for me.

This moment in time felt as if heaven kissed earth as I became aware of God's perfect love, and that is what drew me from my seat to ask Jesus into my heart. It reminds me of Peter's profession of Jesus when asked, "Who do you say I am?" (Matthew 16:15). Peter professed Jesus as the Messiah and Christ. Matthew affirms how God is revealed to us by the Spirit when he wrote, "Blessed are you, Simon son of Jonah, for this was not revealed to you by flesh and blood, but by my Father in heaven" (Matthew 16:17). New life poured into me that day.

That day I gave my life to Christ. It was a big moment and the best moment of my life. Though I felt the next day as if nothing had changed, over time I've grown to know that this walk with Christ is a journey and that my greatest value is being found in him, in being his daughter.

Do you remember when you met Jesus? It may take revisiting that day when you received Christ into your heart—remembering your first love—to truly understand your worth.

Many Protestant churches have a font with water at the sanctuary entrance where people can dip their finger as a tangible act of remembering their baptism. What if there was a tangible way for us to tap into those memories of when we first met Jesus? In 2023, I coauthored a song with two members of our church worship team called "When We Met Jesus." It's about remembering how we felt when we met Jesus, and it's an invitation for others to meet Jesus too and see how he changes everything: "When we met Jesus / he broke off our chains and he freed us / our sin washed away / yeah, he cleaned us / can we tell you how everything changed / when we met Jesus."[4]

It's great to be recognized. It's amazing to be affirmed and appreciated for who we are and what we've done. It's awesome to have nice possessions and to be held in high regard by those around us. But placing our worth in anything other than Christ will always lead us down a path of destruction and leave us feeling empty.

We've always been valuable and worthy of love, period. And we have always been loved by God. He calls us his daughters.

The psalmist in Proverbs 3:15 writes, "She is more precious than rubies." *You* are worth more than rubies. Yet have you experienced times when you felt insignificant? Times when you felt worthless? Have decisions in your past or present influenced how you value yourself? Our actions can be indicators of what we believe about ourselves and what we believe about God. A. W. Tozer is noted for saying, "What comes into our minds when we think about God is the most important thing about us." How do you view yourself? How do you value yourself?

JESUS AND THE SAMARITAN WOMAN

To God, we are more valuable than rubies. We see this in Jesus' encounter with the Samaritan woman in John 4:1-42. The Samaritan woman was known to have had multiple husbands in her past, and the man she was currently with was not her husband. Even today, this woman would be looked down upon by some people in the church world. To add to her plight, Jews disliked Samaritans—they didn't want to be seen near them, let alone talk to them.

Yet when the Samaritan woman comes to draw water from the well that day, Jesus is there and initiates a conversation with her. He invites her to live with him in this grief-filled world. At this point, the woman just wants to draw her water and be done with it. She had planned to come to the well at a time of day when no one else would be there. Have you ever decided to run an errand looking like a hot mess, hoping you don't run into anyone you know, and then you see everybody and their mama? This was that day for the Samaritan woman. Yet, what better person to meet when you feel like a mess than Jesus? To live well in this grief-filled world as Black women, we must go to the well where Jesus is. Jesus doesn't discriminate, nor does he care about our past or the color of our skin. He cares only about the condition of our hearts. He meets us where we are.

The Samaritan woman reminds me of Black women, perhaps because she was a minority. She was looked down upon by others, especially by the Jews. Her past may have influenced her relationships with men, how she viewed herself, and how she interacted with Jesus. When we meet her, she is alone with her thoughts. The location of her encounter with Jesus—Jacob's well in the middle of a desert—reminds us that this land was dry. The well was dug deep to get to the water. Sometimes we have to dig deep to reach the water to get to Jesus.

My Grandma Emma had a ground well at her house. When we visited growing up, the only way to get water was to pump it. We primed the pump by putting in a little water, took the handle, and then lifted it up and down until we felt it catch. Then we pumped until water gushed through the mouth of the pump. Grandma eventually had regular plumbing installed in her home, but having to pump water from that well is a core memory for me.

Drawing water and pumping water from a well are different, but they have the same purpose: to bring water to the surface. Similarly, God draws out our potential from our stumbling blocks, our sins, and our mindsets that keep us stuck. Like a goldsmith who heats metal to bring the impurities to the surface, God sees our true worth and value because he is the discerner of all things. In him, we are his most valuable possession. This well where the Samaritan woman met Jesus never could run dry because she found the Living Water himself.

Let's explore what Jesus does for us when he meets us where we are.

- *He reimages.* God helps the Samaritan woman realize her potential and her worth. He proclaims that whoever drinks from the water he gives will never thirst again (John 4:13-14). God also helps us to realize our potential despite what the culture or anyone else says about us. He offers us his living water that transforms our entire lives. In Christ we find our value and are made new.

- *He reveals.* God reveals who he is to the Samaritan woman (John 4:26). She receives the revelation, not by flesh and blood but by the Spirit, that Jesus is the Messiah. When we encounter Jesus, we receive revelation of who he is: our protector, healer, provider, and defender.

- *He restores.* The Samaritan woman came to the well with shame and left so filled with the gospel that she ran back to her village telling everyone, "Come, see a man who told me everything I ever did" (John 4:29). Those who heard her believed in Jesus because of her testimony. So too does God restore us. Though we may encounter challenges because of who we are and what we've done that has brought us grief, God stands waiting and ready with open arms to forgive and restore us. John wrote, "If we confess our sins, he is faithful and just and will forgive us our sins and purify us from all unrighteousness" (1 John 1:9).

Do you ever feel like you're in a dry place and there's nowhere else to turn? Do you feel as if no one cares? If so, know you are not alone. Jesus wants to not only meet with you but also to reimage you, restore you, and bring revelation of who he is into your life.

JESUS AND THE LEPERS

The story of the lepers in Luke 17:11-19 affirms that God deeply cares about us no matter who we are. Lepers had leprosy, a disease that caused their skin and limbs to rot and smell. It was highly contagious, so they had to live alone—with themselves, with their thoughts, and with their disease. As a result, lepers were outcasts. They were not allowed in places of worship or work and were often separated from their families. When people saw them, the lepers shouted "Unclean! unclean!" (Leviticus 13:45). They had to identify themselves to others as being unclean. Because if by chance others touched the lepers, they would be unclean and have to wash and isolate themselves for some time.

Can you imagine having to shout out and identify yourself as something less than what you really are or someone who God hasn't created you to be? To a society and a culture around you who at times couldn't care less or only made you feel worse? I believe that as Black women we know this feeling. No, we do not have to shout about it, but our skin tones alone speak louder than our words. It's as if it will always go before our words are ever spoken. So as Black women, we might feel like outcasts too. What thoughts do you have when you're isolated from others? Maybe you feel no one cares or understands. Maybe you wonder why this is happening to you.

When I was young, my sister and I once went to our white friend's house to swim in her above-ground pool. We were having so much fun in the cool water on that hot summer day— until our friend's grandma came charging out of the house, shouting, "Get out!" Afraid and shaking, we jumped out and headed home, not knowing what else to do. There were no explanations and no other words said. Afterward, I could only think it was because we were Black and she didn't want Black children in their pool. This was confirmed after we overheard our parents saying it was like our "Black skin would rub off in the water." It made me sad. Our friend was our friend, and color didn't dictate that friendship. Being seen as an outcast because of our skin didn't feel good. This was the life of the lepers, who cried, "Lord, have mercy." How often have we also cried, "Lord, have mercy"?

What we find in the story of the lepers is how Jesus cared for them. He took notice of their plight and stopped to help them, showing that deliverance, salvation, and healing are for everyone. This is the grace and hope we've held since the time of slavery. Though we are cast aside by society, we are not cast aside by God. The apostle Paul wrote, "We are hard pressed on every side, but not crushed; perplexed, but not in despair; persecuted, but not abandoned; struck down, but not destroyed" (2 Corinthians 4:8-9). Have you had times when you felt hard-pressed, like you were stuck between a rock and a hard place? At times do you feel confused, persecuted, or struck down by the weight of grief, pain, and suffering? You may not have enough fingers to count them all. It's so easy to feel any or all of these things in our grief-filled world.

Yet, we can encourage ourselves in the Word of God that we are not crushed, not in despair, not abandoned, and not destroyed. We can have hope knowing God is for us. To him, we're not just another number. Look more deeply into one of the most well-known verses in the Bible: "For God so loved the world that he gave his one and only Son, that *whoever* believes in him shall not perish but have eternal life" (John 3:16, emphasis mine). This tells us we're included.

When it seems as if no one cares about you, know that God truly does. Luke points to how God is intricately concerned about the details of our lives: in caring for the grass and flowers, he cares for us so much more (Luke 12:27-28). Beloved, you are loved and cared for by the Maker of heaven and earth. You and your children and your children's children matter. They always have.

Dear Black woman,

Rest in knowing that you and your Black family are beautifully and wonderfully made by the Creator of the universe. Just as the hairs on your head are delicately counted, and just as he has numbered and named the stars in the sky, so too are the eyes of our Father on you to lovingly care for you throughout your life. He sees and knows all you are going through. He has even captured every tear from your eyes and understands them all without you having to say a word. There's never a moment he doesn't care fully about the things that concern you. Therefore, bring everything to him. And when it feels as if the world doesn't care, know that God does. You matter and your family matters. You are his most valuable possession. You are the apple of his eye.

3

REPRESENTATION MATTERS

The representation of black women is not just about
being seen; it's about being heard, understood,
and respected for the fullness of our humanity.

ANGELA DAVIS

IN THE SPRING OF 2023, I watched my youngest daughter's face light up while we watched the live-action debut of Disney's *The Little Mermaid.* She sat with her eyes glued to the screen, hardly touching her candy or asking for more popcorn as she normally does. Beaming from ear to ear, she said, "Ma, she's brown like me. Her hair is like mine."

"Yes, it is." I smiled. That was the first time I realized the power of representation for my seven-year-old daughter. Yet, unbeknown to her, when Disney announced in July 2019 the lead role of Ariel would go to Halle Bailey, a Black woman, the internet just about broke. There was so much racism and, dare I say, pure evil in comments being posted across the media.

When people take issue with the race of a fictional character, it makes you think we have gotten nowhere.

My sisters and I would get so excited to see anybody who was Black on television when we were growing up, feeling like we made it! I loved seeing Gabby Douglas and Simone Biles in gymnastics. And Serena and Venus Williams in tennis. And the first Black First Lady of the United States, Michelle Obama, and first Black Vice President Kamala Harris. I know that seeing Black women represented on various stages and platforms strongly shapes our belief in ourselves. It gives us confidence that we too can do the same. And it inspires and motivates us to one day be that representation for other Black women.

I had white Barbies and baby dolls growing up. At the time I didn't think much of it. But what were the true implications of being underrepresented in a world that is supposed to have equal rights and equal opportunity? Shouldn't there also be equal representation?

When I read about the first Black solo swimmer, I sent a screenshot to my daughter, who's a swimmer at her school. We were so excited to see representation in her sport. I'm grateful for books like *Crowned with Glory* by Dorena Williamson that help young Black girls appreciate and love their hair. My youngest daughter reads this book at least once a week. *Chasing God's Glory* by Dorina Lazo Gilmore-Young is another wonderful book where we see brown faces on the cover and within its pages.

IMPLICATIONS OF UNDERREPRESENTATION

Being underrepresented as Black women suggests to others that we are less important, less attractive, and not good enough. This perspective can take a huge toll on our self-esteem and confidence. The conversation surrounding the underrepresentation of Black women has been around for as long as I can remember—whether in the media, higher education, health care, STEM, or entertainment. According to the American Psychiatric Association, Black clinicians represent only about 2 percent of practicing psychiatrists and 4 percent of psychologists providing care.[1] Even in the publishing industry, only a little over 15 percent of all authors are Black.[2]

Representation is important because it helps dismantle stereotypes. During Black History Month there is a surge in seeing more Black women in places we normally don't see them. While we are Black women all year long, this month allows us to remember those who have gone before us to pave the way for the opportunities we have today. There are many Black women who represent us well and continue to give us hope as we revisit their phenomenal impact on our country and our lives: Harriet Tubman, Rosa Parks, Maya Angelou, Shirley Chisholm, Madam C. J. Walker, Nina Simone, Angela Davis, Michelle Obama, Oprah Winfrey, Jarena Lee, and Sojourner Truth. And the list goes on. Jane Bolin was the first African American woman to graduate from Yale Law School and the first to serve as a judge in the United States. Bessie Coleman was the first African American to hold an international pilot license. Regina Benjamin was the eighteenth Surgeon General of the United States. And because I'm a writer, I have to mention Ida B. Wells, a journalist and human rights activist who helped to found the National Association for the Advancement of Colored People (NAACP). To celebrate Black History Month, I created flash cards of these famous and not-as-famous Black people, which I've used in homeschooling my young children for many years.

We hope to be inspired by other Black women, and we hope to be an inspiration. So how do we navigate our underrepresentation with hope through the lens of God's Word? I believe we must remember who we are in Christ and understand we are known and approved by God.

GOD'S PURPOSE AND PLAN

God has a purpose and a plan for us all. The prophet Jeremiah proclaims that God knows the plans he has for us, good plans and not evil, to give us an expected end (Jeremiah 29:11). Our part is to trust his plan for our life, even when we cannot find someone who looks like us that points us to his plan and purpose in our world. We still must trust God. In her book *A Sojourner's Truth,* Natasha Sistrunk Robinson helps us reflect on the purpose God has for us: "He often affirms that purpose over time and through our experiences. Our responsibility is to trust God, follow where he leads, and never give up."[3]

Think about the experiences you've had. Whether good or bad, they are all being used to fulfill God's purpose and plan in your life. By knowing who we are as daughters of God, we become representatives for God's kingdom. As the Great Commission says, we should "go and make disciples of all nations, baptizing them in the name of the Father and of the Son and of the Holy Spirit, and teaching them to obey everything I have commanded you" (Matthew 28:19-20), keeping in mind the greatest commandment is to "love the Lord your God with all your heart and with all your soul and with all your mind" (Matthew 22:37).

We become the leaders and influencers we want to see. What is a simple framework for thinking through God's plan for our life? Perhaps it begins with seeking and asking God—believing and trusting in the steps he has already put in place for us.

At the writing of this book, I'm just now feeling as though I'm becoming who God created me to be. And it only took me a whole forty-five years! When I posted about this on social media, I received comments from people both older and younger than I am who still haven't figured it out. Several tools can help us find our natural talents and gifts. But what did Jesus do to walk into God's purpose and plan for his life? He did what the Father told him—and in doing so disappointed a lot of people. Peter Scazzero writes in his book *Emotionally Healthy Spirituality* that because Jesus walked in a maturity of his healthy "true self," he disappointed his family, the people he grew up with, his closest friends, his disciples, and religious leaders.[4] I like to say when we know who we are, no one can tell us who we are not. So Jesus knew his calling, he knew his purpose, and he didn't allow those around him to dictate what he should do or not do based on their expectations of him. As Black women, we can be like Jesus and not let others' expectations dictate how we operate in this world. This position is only designated by our Father in heaven, who is our guide and the ruler of all things.

Loss has helped me move closer to becoming my truest self. Maybe this is the same for you. Perhaps loss and grief have stripped away layers to reveal more of who you truly are. And maybe you've lost people along the way in that revealing—maybe family, maybe friends, maybe ministry leaders, like Jesus did.

TAP INTO YOUR TRUEST SELF
(ADAPTED FOR BLACK WOMEN)

There are ways to practice walking in our "true selves." Here are four ideas, adapted from *Emotionally Healthy Spirituality*, that we can begin tapping into.[5]

1. *Pay attention to your inner voice.* We most often believe our own voice above anyone else's. Take time to sit with your emotions and process them. Through the psalmist, God encourages us to "be still, and know that I am God" (Psalm 46:10). He is with us and will help guide us through our emotions.

2. *Find trusted friends.* I'm a true believer in finding your people, your tribe. We heal within a community of like-minded individuals: those who understand, who don't judge or try to fix us but can tell us hard truths in love, and who come alongside us on the journey. Ecclesiastes 4:9-10 says, "Two are better than one, because they have a good return for their labor: If either of them falls down, one can help the other up. But pity anyone who falls and has no one to help them up."

3. *Move out of your comfort zone.* Change and growth happen outside of our comfort zone. Sometimes this means challenging things we've always believed in and placing those beliefs side-by-side with the Word of God, letting the truth fall where it falls. Joshua wrote, "Have I not commanded you? Be strong and courageous. Do not be afraid; do not be discouraged, for the LORD your God will be with you wherever you go" (Joshua 1:9).

4. *Pray for courage.* Change is hard even when we are taking steps toward Christ. Even when we're trying to become who we are meant to be. That's why prayer is our faithful friend. Paul wrote, "For the Spirit God gave us does not make us timid, but gives us power, love and self-discipline" (2 Timothy 1:7). Pray for courage when the fear rises that we will never be who God called us to be or when others' opinions start to ring in our ears. May our prayers for courage silence all the noise.[6]

ESTHER'S STORY OF REPRESENTATION

Esther's story of resistance and courage in the Bible is a great example of the impact of representing our people. The story begins by introducing King Xerxes, ruler over 127 provinces stretching from India to Cush (Esther 1:1). He throws a huge banquet to celebrate the third year of his reign. On the seventh day of the banquet, he requests Queen Vashti to come to him wearing her royal crown to display her beauty to everyone, but she refuses. As a result, she is stripped of her crown and forbidden to ever see the king again—revealing the consequences for any woman of nobility who acts in such a rebellious manner. With the queen removed from her position, a search is on for a new queen. This turns out to be Esther, a Jew and an orphan raised by her cousin Mordecai.

In reading Esther's story, I immediately noticed that Mordecai forbids her from revealing her nationality and family background, which is mentioned on two occasions in Esther 2:10 and 2:20. This is for good reason, as Haman, a noble of King Xerxes, is leading a plot to kill all the Jews in Susa where Esther lives. Haman's plot demonstrates a hatred toward others simply based on their race, nationality, or background. Unlike Esther, we can't hide our Blackness. Most often our skin tones and shades of brown are an indication that we are Black women.

Fear spreads across the land because of Haman's plot. Mordecai asks Esther to approach the king about this, but a decree proclaims that anyone who approaches the king without being summoned will be put to death unless the king extends his gold scepter to them and spares their life (Esther 4:11). This reminds me of the many ways we as Black women are prevented from showing up due to discrimination, family expectations, fear, and prejudice. How many times have we been left out of the conversation because of our Blackness?

As Esther's story continues, it becomes clear that God has placed her where she is for a purpose. Because of all that is happening in their land, Mordecai warns her, "For if you remain silent at this time, relief and deliverance for the Jews will arise from another place, but you and your father's family will perish.

And who knows but that you have come to your royal position for such a time as this?" (Esther 4:14). Sometimes it's easier to stay quiet to avoid ruffling any feathers. Sometimes our very existence is disturbing to others. Thankfully, Esther does not stay quiet and decides to look to God for help. She tells the people to come together and fast for her, recognizing there is power in unity. I believe fasting does not move the hand of God but instead moves our hearts toward his. Esther says, "When this is done, I will go to the king, even though it is against the law. And if I perish, I perish" (Esther 4:16).

When Queen Esther comes before the king, he accepts her, and she arranges a meeting to reveal Haman's scheme of killing the Jews. She then requests the king to spare her people, declaring, "For I and my people have been sold to be destroyed, killed and annihilated. If we had merely been sold as male and female slaves, I would have kept quiet, because no such distress would justify disturbing the king" (Esther 7:4).

Esther saves a nation with courage and resistance through full reliance on the Lord. As Black women, we are modern day Esthers, because we can petition the King of kings for our people. We can call a fast, we can pray, and we can come boldly before the throne and receive grace. When things happen in our communities, the often-resounding response is that thoughts and prayers are not enough. I get the sentiment, but you ain't about to tell me that prayer doesn't work. Prayer does bring change. And some things only come through prayer and fasting. So let us be the Esthers of our time.

You were created for such a time as this.

Dear Black woman,

You may long to see someone who looks just like you in all the places you aspire to be in. Or you may long to see another Black woman achieve new heights to inspire you and the next generation. You may long to be represented in your church and your circles of influence, yet you find yourself wanting. I encourage you to be the representation you want to see. I encourage you to be God's representation everywhere you go, pursuing his plan and purpose for you on earth. To use your unique qualities, gifts, and talents for God's glory. To help others see the goodness of God in and through you so they will know him for themselves. To influence those around you like Esther by simply representing Jesus wherever you go. Let your presence be his presence in the here and now.

4

ENOUGH IS ENOUGH

*To bring about change, you must not be afraid to take
the first step. We will fail when we fail to try.*

ROSA PARKS

GROWING UP, MY FAMILY WAS POOR. But it didn't feel like
it to me. I remember going to my childhood medical checkups
and hurrying over to the toy area to play with several other kids
waiting to be seen by the doctor. I thought it was kind of fun.
The people were nice there. Later in life, I would accompany
my sister Sharon with her first child to the same place: the
county health department.

It was a service provided to county residents regardless of
their age and ability to pay. But it was just the doctor's office to
me. These visits took us through our younger years, and as we
got older, we'd only go to the doctor for emergencies. My first
visit to a dentist was when I landed my first job with benefits
out of college. Praise the Lord, Mom taught us good hygiene.

After twenty-one years of never seeing a dentist, I can say with a smile that I have only ever had one cavity.

We periodically went to New Bern, a bigger town in our county, to stand in line for a free box of food. I didn't think anything of it at the time. Now I understand my parents used this opportunity to stretch the food budget. In my younger years, I also accompanied my mom several times to the unemployment office. As a seamstress in a dying fabric and apparel manufacturing industry, she experienced numerous temporary layoffs. Being laid off wasn't my mom's fault. But this was where we were.

To complicate things, my dad developed health issues in his early forties. With both parents working intermittently, our family of six needed assistance. I've found that we don't all receive the same start in life. We are not all privy to all the resources at any given time, nor do we all have family to act as a safety net when things get hard.

I came to realize my family was part of the government assistance program, also known as welfare. I didn't realize this until my high school years when we no longer needed the assistance and I started hearing other people talk about those who were on government assistance. My childhood experience reminds me of the classic Black sitcom *Good Times*. The show was set in the 1970s and featured the Evans family living in government housing in Chicago and doing their best to survive hard times.

My family could relate to the Evans family. We found ourselves somewhere in the plot of each episode, whether the characters were scraping up money to make a house payment, dealing with racial violence and discrimination, experiencing layoffs, you name it. My family went through it all firsthand.

BROKEN SYSTEMS

Many systems in our world inform our quality of life and the way we live. As Black women, we find ourselves navigating the consequences of broken systems, such as the following:

- Higher poverty and government assistance rates within our financial system
- Higher incarceration rates within the justice system
- Higher mortality rates within the health care system
- Higher unequal opportunity rates for education and employment within our institutional system

The thread that connects these broken systems is structural and systemic racism, two different types of racism that appear subtly in our everyday lives. Toni Morrison once said, "In this country American means white. Everybody else has to hyphenate."[1] This idea further delineates how race is a significant factor in our country's various systems. I admit I didn't always understand the differences between structural and systemic racism, so I'll describe them here:

Systemic racism emphasizes the involvement of whole systems, and often all systems—for example, political, legal, economic, health care, school, and criminal justice systems, including the structures that uphold the systems.

> *Structural racism* emphasizes the role of the structures (laws, policies, institutional practices, and entrenched norms) that are the system's scaffolding.
>
> *Institutional racism* is sometimes used as a synonym for systemic or structural racism, as it captures the involvement of institutional systems and structures in race-based discrimination and oppression.[2]

We were born into a world that operates on systems that weren't created for us. As a result, navigating through this life can often feel like wading through quicksand with concrete boots. It can sometimes feel otherworldly.

The term *otherworldly* makes me think of the Marvel Cinematic Universe (MCU) multiverse. If you are familiar with that term, you are my people. In *Spider-Man: Into the Spider-Verse*, Black teenager Miles Morales lives a double life as Spider-Man, who his dad, a police officer, views as a menace. Miles gets thrown into other dimensions, or universes, and teams up with the other Spider-Man versions to defeat the villain.

Facing the things we face as Black women can make it seem like we're living in different worlds too. And just when we think we've halfway figured it out, the rules change.

"We all get the same start in life" and "I don't see color" are phrases I heard my white male pastor say as I sat in the congregation of a church I no longer attend. Honestly, I haven't been able to shake these statements even after some years. I felt so many emotions after hearing them, from sadness to anger to disappointment to mere shock. I wanted to ask

him, "Was slavery the same start in life for everyone?" We
all know this is a resounding no. In trying to make sense of
how someone in ministry—particularly a pastor of a mixed
congregation—could make such statements, I learned that his
views reflected colorblindness.

Psychology Today notes *colorblindness* is the racial ideology
that says treating individuals equally, without regard to race,
culture, or ethnicity, is the best way to eliminate discrimination. However, not only does this view fail to heal racial
wounds, but it even functions as a form of racism.[3] So even
the well-meaning can do more harm than good. Sadly, I truly
believe the pastor meant no harm. He intended to make space
for the topic of racial injustice happening in our country by
bringing his insight and maybe even connecting with Black
congregants. Instead, Black congregants ended up feeling
more unseen, unheard, misunderstood, and hurt, including
myself. I believe teachers, preachers, pastors, and leaders
need more training and education on the trauma and grief
surrounding matters of race, especially non-Black pastors of
mixed congregations.

Black, Indigenous, and other people of color (BIPOC)
didn't have the "same start" as white people—and for Black
people, the root causes are chattel slavery, Black Codes, and the
Jim Crow laws. Chattel slavery, the most known form of slavery,
meant one person was the legal property of another person.[4]
Black Codes, put into place after the Civil War ended, allowed
Black people certain rights but denied us rights in other areas.
Jim Crow laws created limitations on the daily lives of Black

people. Issued in the late 1800s, these laws were passed to re-inforce segregation by way of separating Black and white people in transportation, schools, theaters, parks, restaurants, etc.[5]

For 246 years, from 1619 to 1865, most Black people were enslaved, unable to own property and make a living. While we were subjected to unpaid labor and unfair treatment, slave owners were storing money, land, and wealth for themselves and their heirs.[6] It's crazy that this is part of our story. We weren't afforded the time or the opportunity to gain wealth, which put us behind financially and in so many other ways for generations to come. The few Black people who were able to make a living angered their white counterparts so much they were met with violence, death, and punishment. Unfortunately, the same is true today in some cases.

We often hear that our country was built on the foundation of the Word of God. While this sounds beautiful, Black people are all too aware that our country's founders were slave owners—which means our foundation is not as firm as people think. This continues the conversation about faulty systems. Because of what we've heard and witnessed, we are skeptical of world systems. We flat out don't trust "the system." As a result, we are more reluctant to ask for help when we are facing hardships or experiencing medical or mental health issues. We've been taught to believe the church should help us in these areas, but the thing is, churches are broken too. Most of our churches are not equipped with grief- or trauma-informed individuals. Many churches attempt to counsel with good intentions, yet they can only speak from the limited view of their own experiences.

While experience is important, we cannot let it be our only guide. The Word of God must be first and foremost to lead and guide us in these areas. And where available, relevant research, training, and tools can help as well.

THE HEALTH CARE SYSTEM

We are inferior in the eyes of our society and culture, which adds to the mental health challenges we face. Research suggests more Black women are diagnosed with mental illness than Black men, yet our use of health services is low.[7] Dealing with mental health challenges has often been stigmatized within our communities. Growing up, I would hear rumors about people who were sent to Cherry Hospital, a mental institution several hours away from my hometown. Those individuals were called "crazy." It's sad to think about now, because when we know better, we do better. So much harm was done to Black women in our communities who didn't have the support they needed from their families, friends, and even the church. All because of miscommunication, ignorance, and fear.

In addition, a sociopolitical history involving trauma and victimization of African Americans has served to foster cultural mistrust toward the US health care system.[8] We don't trust the system because it has not been good or fair to us. From the outside looking in, it's easy to say Black women are using the system. But the truth is, I've never personally known a Black woman to think or say, "I just love having to depend on the system." It's been the total opposite.

Black women are two to three times more likely than white women to die of pregnancy-related causes.[9] Having personally known a Black woman who died only hours after giving birth, it makes me ask how this happens and why it's so prevalent among Black women. To add to our fear surrounding the medical system, in the early 1900s "a medical doctor named Harry J. Haiselden preyed on Black mothers and openly admitted to news media and medical journals that he allowed Black babies to die based on his eugenic beliefs."[10] This is a part of our history that makes my skin crawl.

The practice of Black women getting their tubes tied as a temporary sterilization of their reproductive system can be traced back to the time of chattel slavery when Black women were treated like livestock and cattle. Slave owners had control over their reproduction. Doctors experimented to keep the fertile women fertile and took drastic measures to "fix" those who were not. Black women who were not able to have children were often mistreated and abused because their infertility meant a loss of money for the slave owner.

In the early 1900s, laws were passed in several states that authorized the sterilization of women. This later became forced sterilizations that targeted low-income Black women to reduce the number eligible for public assistance. Again, how did this happen? Social factors do not protect Black women, especially when they are ignored by the health care system and their pain is dismissed. This invisibility, caused by bias, discrimination, and racism from health care providers, leads to higher rates of maternal death and health problems for Black women.[11]

So how do we help promote change? Health care providers need proper training to create a fair and unbiased system for people of color. Providers should be sensitive to and respectful of diverse cultures. Additionally, a more diverse and culturally aware workforce will help meet the unique needs of Black women, improving maternal health.[12] Several organizations are leading the way in this area, including the Black Mamas Matter Alliance (BMMA), the National Birth Equity Collaborative (NBEC), and the Association of Black Women Physicians (ABWP). These are all organizations that advocate for the advancement of Black maternal health, rights, and justice and work with policymakers to address structural inequities.

THE JUSTICE SYSTEM

Research suggests that "although people of color represent 39 percent of the US population, they make up over 60 percent of incarcerated people" and "nearly one in three Black men will be imprisoned, and nearly half of all Black women currently have a family member or extended family member who is in prison."[13] Not all Black women have experienced injustice, but we most likely know someone who has. Higher incarceration rates can be traced back to Jim Crow and Black Codes, which targeted Black people, subjected them to harsh treatment, and limited their opportunities.

The PBS documentary *Slavery by Another Name* sheds light on why these superficial laws, codes, and structures were put in place: because of the amount of wealth that many states in this country were accumulating at the expense of Black people's lives and livelihoods. The documentary notes how our freedom came with a cost, as it devastated the Southern economy, particularly the cotton economy. So even though emancipation had taken place, Black people were still targeted and criminalized. Convict leasing was a system of forced labor used as another avenue akin to slavery to exploit Black people, where prisoners were leased out by the government to business owners, though many Black people within the system were convicted of ambiguous or subjective crimes.[14]

In December 2014, the African American Policy Forum and the Center for Intersectionality and Social Policy Studies launched the #SayHerName campaign, which "brings awareness to the often invisible names and stories of Black women and girls who have been victimized by racist police violence." Since then, the related phrase "say their names" and the hashtag #SayTheirNames have been invoked to recognize Black victims of police violence more broadly.[15] This initiative was one of the first of its kind to recognize Black women victims. Black women are often overlooked, as headlines of Black men fill our feeds. Breonna Taylor's story sent a surge of fear through the Black community because it was a devastating demonstration that Black women are not safe anywhere.

How do we live above broken systems? Some even better questions are: How do we live through broken systems if they are meant to keep us down? Given what we know about these systems, what do we do? In the Bible we find examples of injustices and we see resistance against those who have done no wrong due to race and status, like the children of Israel who were held in slavery for years and years.

THE DAUGHTERS OF ZELOPHEHAD

One example is the story of the daughters of Zelophehad in Numbers 27. Mahlah, Noah, Hoglah, Milcah, and Tirzah's father has died, and up until this time only sons inherited possessions after a father's death. Their grief is unmistakable—they have lost their father, there is no mention of their mother in the story, and they are moving into another land with next to nothing. When we lose a parent, we also encounter many secondary losses, including loss of security, loss of possession, and loss of identity. Surely these women experienced this as well. But instead of letting the dice roll, they decided to ask for their inheritance. It was still theirs to have, but a technicality was keeping them from it.

The daughters of Zelophehad come before Moses and the other leaders to tell them that their father died and had no sons. They then courageously go further to make their case: "Why should our father's name disappear from his clan because he had no son? Give us property among our father's relatives" (Numbers 27:4). Get this: this is the first example in Scripture of women demanding their rights. It makes me think again how women have been at a disadvantage from the beginning of time, since sin entered the world. That's why it is encouraging to learn about our forerunners who led the way to change and freedom.

What's more, God affirms these daughters' rights. "Moses brought their case before the LORD, and the LORD said to him,

'What Zelophehad's daughters are saying is right. You must certainly give them property as an inheritance among their father's relatives and give their father's inheritance to them'" (Numbers 27:5-7). Because of these women's courage, the law was changed to include daughters as worthy inheritors.

This reminds us that the Lord is before all things and in all things. It reminds us that we can come boldly before the Lord in prayer to make our petitions known. It reminds us that the Lord is the one who orchestrates lasting change and that ultimately, this world is not our home.

Dear Black woman,

Feeling broken while living in a broken world can lead us to feel hopeless. I've found myself here a few too many times, whether I was being overlooked or feeling the heartbreak of those nearest and dearest to me who have been hurt by the broken systems they were part of.

The broken systems of this world try to keep us from seeing our true potential and discourage us from being all God has called us to be. No, we do not get the same start in life, yet because Jesus came to give us life to the full, we can tap into the resources we have in Christ.

Though you may feel broken at times, you certainly are not broken beyond repair. The kingdom of God lives within you, which means your life has a greater purpose than you could ever imagine. Each one of us can flip the script and change the narrative for ourselves, our children, and the next generation.

5

COURAGEOUS FAITH

*The world is a severe schoolmaster, for its frowns are
less dangerous than its smiles and flatteries, and it is
a difficult task to keep on the path of wisdom.*

PHILLIS WHEATLEY

DURING A CONVERSATION with one of my non-Black
friends about how I was feeling writing this book, she said,
"Well, it doesn't seem like your family has any problems with
racial issues."

I got what she was saying. From the outside looking in,
yes, my husband and our kids are blessed not to have directly
dealt with racial violence. Yet, I think this proves a point that it
doesn't have to happen to me for it to matter to me—because it
has the potential to happen to me and those I love.

I still experience subtle forms of racial bias, such as being
overlooked for being a Black woman. What's more, I bear
witness throughout these pages to the grief my family has experienced and the grief that still may come. As a writer, especially

as a Black writer, my words can be taken the wrong way out of context. I once received a one-star review on my first book, *Can You Just Sit with Me.* The reviewer suggested that my book made them feel bad to be white and that I had a political agenda because I mentioned the grief that Black people felt heavily during the pandemic of 2020. I experienced hesitation while writing this book because talking about anything dealing with race often leads to raised eyebrows. People seem to ask, *Why can't you write a book that includes us all?*

One thing is for certain: as Black women, "suffering comes with the territory." I got this poignant phase from fellow author Paul Borthwick after reading his book *The Fellowship of Suffering* and chatting with him on my podcast.[1] He was referring to what it means to suffer with and for Christ as a Christian. But it made me think of how this phrase relates to Black women. We were not assigned to suffering; we were born into it.

A constant grief rests like dew on our lives. It often feels as if our own grief weighs more heavily than anyone else's because we are the ones experiencing it. Yet because we're born into this broken world as Black women, we tolerate *a lot.* From personal experience, I believe I have a high tolerance to pain—or maybe it's because I numb myself to not feel the full brunt of it. I wonder if our grief can be measured to reveal the impact of world events, our own trauma, and other factors on our lives. While we share collective grief experiences, no two people grieve in the same way.

Many Black women report being in a constant state of mourning. We are having to constantly process and adapt to life after loss as we endlessly witness the deaths of our people through the news and social media.

The week I wrote this chapter, there was another racially motivated killing of three Black people, this time in Jacksonville, Florida. The tragic reality is that by the time you read this chapter, this event will already exist in the shadow of many other events like it.

It begs the question again and again: *Why?* And why us?

My heart hurts so badly over this loss and those past. I've sat with my thoughts but had no words. And there still aren't words to soothe the ache we feel as Black women for our communities when we are assaulted by the news of yet another senseless murder.

We are left with the same question: "When will it stop?" It feels as if we are shouting into the wind only for our words to be carried off into the abyss. It's so sad to me. If you're sad about it too, know that I'm here with you. You're not alone. And God is with us.

MOURNING AS REBELLION

The murder of Emmett Till in 1955 showed that Black mourning is a form of rebellion. While visiting his family in Mississippi, fourteen-year-old Emmett Till was kidnapped and brutally murdered by white men. His mother, Mamie, decided on an open casket funeral, allowing his mutilated body to be seen by fifty thousand onlookers in Chicago and others across the country through photos displayed in *Jet Magazine*. Video from Emmett's funeral shows crowds of people lined up to view his body; many had to be assisted out of the building because they were going to faint.[2] Journalist Rose Jourdain said, "I think Black people's reaction was so visceral; everybody knew that we were under attack and it was symbolized by the attack on a 14-year-old boy."[3] The fact that public Black mourning was seen as an insult at the time made it even more powerful, as there were some—including Carolyn Pike, the wife of one of his murderers—who believed Emmett's death was a just cause.[4]

The book *Emmett Till: The Murder That Shocked the World and Propelled the Civil Rights Movement* discusses the reminders and words of warning Emmett's mother gave him the last time she saw him alive. Mamie told him if anything was to happen in Mississippi, he was to get on his knees and beg for forgiveness if needed. She said, "No matter how much it seems that you have the right, just forget your rights while you're in Mississippi."[5] This reminds me of "the talk" that we must have even now with our kids. This is why we tell our children humility is everything. My husband says it over and over: "Even if you think you are right, be respectful."

Emmett suffered a death that no one should ever have to suffer. His mother knew she needed to bring light to the darkness. Thus, with no justice in sight, Mamie took matters into her own hands and continued to fight for justice and closure. Having the open casket at Emmett's funeral caught global attention and shed light on the violence taken against this young boy, speaking louder than words ever could.

Evil lurks in the dark. It lies and convinces itself that it is not evil, like Satan who disguises himself as an angel of light

(2 Corinthians 11:14). The apostle John says of the devil, "He was a murderer from the beginning, not holding to the truth, for there is no truth in him. When he lies, he speaks his native language, for he is a liar and the father of lies" (John 8:44).

There is something wrong when people are offended that we mourn the loss of someone in our community. To not mourn is to devalue the life that was taken. I will never forget listening to a pastor in the pulpit make excuses as to why George Floyd was apprehended by police and offer commentary on Floyd's alleged background—instead of extending condolences and just listening to Black members within the church who were hurting. Even Emmett Till's murderer Roy Bryant said, years later after his case was reopened for investigation in 1992, "Why can't people leave the dead alone and quit trying to stir things up?"[6]

NAVIGATING CONSTANT GRIEF

As Black women, we are mourning either our own experience or something going on in the Black community. It's a constant resurgence of grief and pain. It's like navigating through broken glass or a fire. In these cases, we take precautions. We have to ask ourselves which way we're going and what we'll do to get out of it. We either call for help, wait for help to come, or try to make our way to safety. We actively search for ways to make it through as unscathed as possible.

What can be done about Black women's constant grief? I've found that we—referring to anyone who has ever suffered a loss in life—don't get over grief, instead as individuals we experience different outcomes. One is the concept of "growing around grief" as explained by Tonkin's model of grief. Lois Tonkin, an Australian grief counselor, presented the idea of growing around grief when she heard a woman describe her journey of grief processing after losing a child.[7]

I think about how our lifelong experiences with racism and injustice as Black Americans have never gone away, yet we have learned to grow around that type of grief. The same goes for everyone: nothing can change what happened or is happening in our world, nor our associated grief, but we have found ways to grow around it. Though racism still exists, we press on; though natural disasters still happen, we persevere; though national and global tragedies still occur, we find a way through.

Black women especially must adapt due to the onslaught of ongoing grief we experience. Because the grief remains, it seems as if there is no acceptance stage. Trouble is always expected. Consider these three things that cause a constant feeling of grief: anticipatory grief, feeling othered, and disenfranchised grief. We'll take a look at each one.

Anticipatory grief is the process of grieving that starts before a loved one passes. It is the realization on a conscious or unconscious level that a loss is coming.[8] I would go further to say that the process of grieving begins before any loss. Black women may suffer from anticipatory grief when it comes to how society views us because of our color. This is huge and can play out at any place, at any time, and it may even inform our work and our decision-making. As Black women, we can easily anticipate being judged because of our skin color rather than our intellect and the way we dress or wear our hair.

Othering also causes a constant feeling of grief. This is a social process of marginalization through which a person highly values their group while denigrating and excluding anyone from a group different than theirs.[9] I experienced this in the workplace among an increasing population of Spanish-speaking people. As my colleagues became connected like a family, I felt as if I were on the outside looking in. I didn't even know it was possible to feel this way among other minorities.

In her book *Young, Gifted, and Black*, Sheila Wise Rowe says that "people of color sometimes engage in defensive othering. By demonstrating that they share the same attitudes and disdain toward co-ethnics who fit with the stereotypes, they attempt to join the dominant group."[10]

So as Black women, we may feel othered even by other Black women at times. Here are three signs of othering:

1. *Avoiding encounters.* Imagine you're a student at a diverse high school where students naturally segregate themselves during lunchtime based on factors like race, ethnicity, or social cliques. You notice that some students consistently avoid sitting with or interacting with peers who belong to different racial or social groups. For instance, a group of students might actively avoid sitting at tables where students from different racial backgrounds are seated, preferring to stick to their own group. This avoidance of interaction reinforces social divisions within the school and perpetuates stereotypes and prejudices, ultimately hindering opportunities for meaningful cross-cultural exchange and understanding.

2. *Feeling mistrust.* Imagine living in a close-knit neighborhood where everyone knows each other well. One
day, a new family moves in, and they come from a different socioeconomic background than most residents.
Despite their friendly attempts to engage with neighbors,
you notice some residents expressing skepticism and
mistrust toward the new family solely based on their
perceived differences in wealth or social status. They
may gossip about them, avoid interacting with them, or
make assumptions about their character without getting
to know them personally. This suspicion and mistrust
creates barriers to building community cohesion and can
make the new family feel isolated and unwelcome in their
new environment.

3. *Making generalized statements.* Suppose you're in a
classroom discussion about a complex social issue, such
as poverty or crime rates in urban areas. During the discussion, a student makes a generalized statement like,
"People from low-income neighborhoods are more likely
to commit crimes." This statement oversimplifies a multifaceted issue and unfairly stereotypes individuals based on
their socioeconomic status. It fails to consider the under-
lying factors contributing to crime, such as systemic
inequality, lack of access to resources, and historical injustices. Making such generalized statements can perpetuate
negative stereotypes and contribute to the stigmatization
of marginalized communities. Consider asking why this
is important.[11]

Did any of these resonate with you? One thing I've found on this grief journey is that self-awareness is so important. So if something resonated with you, it's not a bad thing but an opportunity to learn more about yourself.

Lastly, *disenfranchised grief* is another reason why Black women are in a constant or resurgent state of grief. This refers to the grief we have silenced because a loss is not deemed worthy by society to be grieved. Factors contributing to disenfranchised grief may include the normalization and dismissal of the grief or trauma endured, the denial of opportunities for proper mourning, and the effects of intersecting identities.[12] If we openly talk about our race-related grief, specifically among our white brothers and sisters, it is often brushed off as if it doesn't matter. We are told we should just be grateful for everything else we have and move on. We may even receive backlash. Robert Neimeyer and John Jordan propose that empathic failures—"the failure of one part of a system to understand the meaning and experience of another"—are central to the construct of disenfranchised grief.[13] This idea of empathic failures fits the framing of Black women's grief, as society as a whole has failed to understand the grief that comes along with simply being born a Black woman.

However, we have a right to grieve—and we must. I pray this book offers permission to grieve every loss you've experienced as a Black woman. There is a history of others trying to silence our grief, because it brings attention to the injustice that continues to happen in our world. Thus, to grieve is to participate in resistance and even open a gateway to awareness and change.

BITTERNESS MEETS ACCEPTANCE

I want to encourage us to not become bitter in this constant state of grief. Our hearts and spirits may grow weary because we have to keep enduring it, for "hope deferred makes the heart sick" (Proverbs 13:12). I remember feeling like God was out to get me. After experiencing loss after loss, I couldn't help but feel like I was the only one going through it. Sometimes we feel like this when it keeps happening to us. Yet, we must guard our hearts against bitterness.

I was nudged several years back to do a personal Bible study on bitterness because I knew I was feeling some kind of way about the succession and weight of grief. Grief never ends because sin will not end until Jesus returns. Grief can turn even the strongest of us in our faith to become bitter. Given this, how do we become better, not bitter? I came to be more aware of the words coming out of my mouth, which told me the state of my being—for out of the abundance of the heart, the mouth speaks (Luke 6:45 ESV). I found myself ruminating on the insurmountable losses I'd incurred and saying cynical things like, "What's the point of trying?" I believe cynicism is the alarm that woke me up to my bitterness. As the writer of Hebrews warns, "Looking carefully lest there be any man that falleth short of the grace of God; lest any root of bitterness springing up trouble you, and thereby the many be defiled" (Hebrews 12:15 ASV).

We can't let what is happening around us get inside us. Bitterness is a feeling or behavior of anger, hurt, or resentment because of one's bad experiences or a sense of unjust treatment. Hebrews 12:15 says that bitterness springs up trouble and produces destructive fruit in our lives. Destructive fruit is the opposite of that mentioned in Galatians: "But the fruit of the Spirit is love, joy, peace, forbearance, kindness, goodness, faithfulness, gentleness and self-control" (Galatians 5:22-23).

Let's pause here. Take a quick assessment using these statements to see if you might have some bitterness underneath the surface.

1. You think you deserve more than you get—in life and love.
2. You don't feel satisfied with your present achievements.
3. You think everyone is out to get you.
4. You don't appreciate how good people treat you.
5. You don't acknowledge other people's skills.
6. It's hard for you to congratulate your friends on their success.
7. You communicate to criticize, not to engage.
8. You dislike cheerful and confident individuals.[14]

Did anything resonate here? If so, it's okay. Self-awareness is a jumping-off point to healing.

Elizabeth Kubler-Ross is known for the five stages of grief based on her work studying death and dying. The stages include denial, anger, bargaining, depression, and acceptance. To the grieving, acceptance is such an ugly word. But as it relates to a Black woman's grief, perhaps it can become a friend. And if we allow acceptance to become part of our language, perhaps it can serve us well.

I usually do not think about acceptance in relation to the many losses I and other Black women have faced. Yet I'm

curious about what would happen if we accepted that this is
the way it is and it will likely not change in our lifetime. It bears
saying that this can make it all seem a bit hopeless. But should
we live in a false reality? The answer is no. More than one thing
can be true at the same time. We can grieve *and* still have hope.
A goal of this book is to help us face this grief-filled world in
such a way that Christ leads and guides us to him, the author
of all hope.

I love how Mary-Frances O'Connor, author of *The Grieving
Brain*, frames acceptance. She says,

> Avoiding the overwhelming feelings of grief, motivated
> by how much you hate those feelings, requires effort. Ac-
> cepting, on the other hand, does not have any bearing on
> whether or not you hate the fact that your loved one died.
> It simply acknowledges the reality and stops the reaction
> here. No ruminating, no problem solving, no anger, no
> protest—just accepting the way it is.[15]

This may be something we already do. A news headline of
another shooting in the Black community flashes across the TV
screen, and we accept that this is the way it is in this country.
But we must also ask what we can do to change this for our
children, our families, and our communities. Michael Jackson
encouraged us in his song "Heal the World" to make the world
a better place for the entire human race. Can we?

What do you think it might feel or sound like to accept things
as they are? What does it look like to have hope in Christ even
when the world seems like it's against us?

The opposite of acceptance is *resistance*, which is defined as the act of fighting against something that is attacking us, or refusing to accept something.[16] Resisting our feelings of loss does not fix the situation. So how can accepting what has happened and will continue to happen be helpful to us? It doesn't mean that what happened was okay. Instead, I believe leaning into acceptance in a hopeful way is courageous because it means having real, honest conversations with ourselves, our families, and our kids to declare this is our world—no matter how messy, broken, and flat-out wrong it is. We will be all right because God is here.

Once we do this, we can say, "Lord, help me to navigate this. How can I be your hands and feet on this earth? How can I help my family, my children, my Black sisters?" We can also admit, "This is hard. This feels insurmountable. This is hopeless without you. Yet you, Lord, know the end from the beginning and give wisdom to those who ask, so we ask for your wisdom even now."

How do we fight the good fight of faith with courage? The short answer is: with and in Christ, for then we can walk faithfully with God amid constant grief and in the face of trials and tribulations.

WHEN TRIALS AND TRIBULATIONS COME

In this life, we will have trouble. The Bible's resolution is to put our trust and faith in God, knowing our trials and tribulations are working in us a far more exceeding and eternal weight in glory (2 Corinthians 4:17). Paul wrote, "We also glory in our sufferings, because we know that suffering produces perseverance; perseverance, character; and character, hope" (Romans 5:3-4). Yes, this life is full of many trials by fire.

We see this in Paul's story. His life was filled with heartache and pain, which included being beaten, put in prison, and stoned. Yet, his life was also filled with God. As Black women, we can glean much from Paul's story while asking ourselves, *What is needed to withstand so much trial?* For one thing, we can remember we are God's—we are daughters of the King. John encourages us: "Yet to all who did receive him, to those who believed in his name, he gave the right to become children of God" (John 1:12).

It is said comparison is the thief of joy. But sometimes comparison helps us to put things in perspective. When we look at Paul's life, he experienced so much suffering. This acknowledgment isn't about minimizing our pain and suffering but about nudging us in our faith. At first, we may be conditioned to think that if Paul experienced so many hard things and was able to press through, then we can too. However, I don't think this wording is helpful. Instead of pressing through, I want to encourage you to lean into God, to rest in him, to call on him, to pray to him, and to sit with him.

Peter wrote,

These trials will show that your faith is genuine. It is being tested as fire tests and purifies gold—though your faith is far more precious than mere gold. So when your faith remains strong through many trials, it will bring you much

praise and glory and honor on the day when Jesus Christ
is revealed to the whole world. (1 Peter 1:7 NLT)

We are often crying out, "How long, Lord?" And it's a valid
cry. In becoming acquainted with long-suffering, we sometimes
make it look too easy. Yet long-suffering is a fruit of the Spirit,
lived out by both the apostle Paul and Jesus.

Dear Black woman,

*God knows the grief that assaults you like fiery darts.
He is aware of the attacks against your heart and
your mind. He has provided his armor to guard
against it. And he has given himself to us to cope
with the hurt of it all. He has given us a community
to walk through it. He has given us a plan and
a purpose to help others as we live for him and the
kingdom. In our every weakness, he is our strength.
We are being made strong in and through him and
nothing in and of ourselves. Every headline, every
experience of inequality, every racial interaction,
every othered experience, every moment of pain from
seeing our loved ones die at higher rates than others—
God sees, he knows, and he understands. A suffering Savior who we serve in turn serves us and our
hurting, grieving hearts. He is our beautiful Savior
who knows what we need and knows the very intent
of our hearts through and through.*

6

THIS IS FREEDOM

You should be angry. You must not be bitter. Bitterness is
like cancer. It eats upon the host. It doesn't do anything
to the object of its displeasure. So use that anger.

You write it. You paint it. You dance it. You march it.

You vote it. You do everything about it.
You talk it. Never stop talking it.

Dr. Maya Angelou

You may be familiar with Bruce Banner, a fictional scientist who gets mutated by gamma rays, which causes him to transform into the Incredible Hulk when he becomes angry. In the movie *The Avengers*, he and a group of other heroes are fighting together in New York City when it looks as if they are outnumbered and are about to be overtaken. Captain America says to Bruce, "Dr. Banner, now might be a really good time for you to get angry." With a smirk, Bruce replies, "That's my secret—I'm always angry."[1]

Our anger can catch us by surprise, which might cause us to push it away instead of examining it further. Yet when we take the time to process our emotions, we may recognize two of the secondary emotions that come with grief: fear and anger. Sometimes our anger is disguised as something else, such as feelings of hurt, passion, or wanting to be heard. Most often, no one stops to ask us if there is something else going on. So in comes the angry Black woman—a stereotype created by society to sear this particular perception of Black women into the minds of those who choose to believe it. In other races, what is perceived as anger in the Black woman might instead be interpreted as strength, the right to assert an opinion, and intelligence.

Research suggests oppressive and controlling roles of Black women were defined by three main stereotypes—the mammy, the jezebel, and the sapphire.[2] The mammy depiction was created to portray Black female house slaves as subservient, fostering a perception of their treatment as acceptable within culture. The jezebel image branded Black women as hypersexual, as a way of justifying sexual abuse and mistreatment. The sapphire image originated with the character from the *Amos 'n' Andy* radio and television show, depicting Black women as overly aggressive and masculinized.

Although the stereotypes exist, they don't discount that we as Black women have things to be angry about. However, it's important to note that our anger may be coming from a place of grief, as anger is part of the grieving process.

ANGER'S PLACE IN GRIEF

Let's revisit the anger stage from the five stages of grief to better think about anger as an emotion of grief. In this stage, people question why something happened and outwardly express anger. If the loss is unpredictable or blindsiding, this stage can be especially difficult.[3] The thing to note is that being angry is not sinful, it's what we do with the anger that matters. In her book *Healing Racial Trauma*, Sheila Wise Rowe wisely informs us, "People of color are justifiably angry about the many injustices we face. The question is what to do with the anger before or after it turns to rage."[4]

Let's identify what anger is and what it is not. Anger is an emotional response and can manifest itself in different ways, including irritation and resentment. It can serve as a protective mechanism, provide energy for action toward a resolution, and signal deeper issues needing attention. Anger is *not* weakness or failure, it's not always destructive or harmful, it's not a solution to problems or conflicts, it's not an excuse for harmful behavior, and it is certainly not a permanent state or identity. If you find yourself angry, don't discount what it may be signifying and most importantly, don't let someone label you because of your anger.

Again, emotions—including anger and fear—are normal. Feelings serve as a form of communication, with anger in particular arising as a natural reaction to perceived harm, mistreatment, or victimization. It indicates a call to action, prompting heightened engagement and mobilization to protect oneself or others. The anger and sense of injustice intertwined with grief present a potent force capable of spurring action to resist injustice. This resilience in the face of sorrow serves a purpose, offering both personal and communal strengths at individual and collective levels.[5] Anger is also part of the healing process.

Some physical symptoms of anger in grief include a tight body, our jaw hurting, stomachaches, a racing mind, an inability to concentrate, and cold or hot sensations.[6]

FEAR'S PLACE IN GRIEF

Fear is also a natural part of life and can sometimes serve as a catalyst for anger. C. S. Lewis's famous line, "No one ever told me that grief felt so like fear," reminds us that grief can cause fear.[7] Like anger, fear is normal. "It is the feeling that results when the defense system is active in a brain that has the capacity for self-awareness."[8] In other words, fear occurs whenever we are threatened.

While anticipatory grief brings fear of what's to come, we also experience fear of the unknown. Fear that we can't keep our loved ones safe. Fear that a particular sickness or disease runs in our family, so we might die from it too. Fear that the world will never change. Fear our neighbor won't love us as they love themselves. Fear our children will be judged, mistreated, and even killed because of the color of their skin. And sometimes fear is not only the death of a relationship but also the death of a dream.

God gave us dominion, yet sometimes we forget that the Bible is not just a white person's Bible, but ours too. Though the Bible has been used against us in the past, this was surely not God's intention.

As Black women, we shrink our true selves to make others around us feel more comfortable. But this keeps us from being who God intended us to be. We often deal with different types of fear, including fear of being unseen or unheard, fear of being misunderstood, and fear of being too much for others. If we are not careful, we walk through life being less than what we could be, should be, or would be. We hold ourselves back, which leads us to experience imposter syndrome.

IMPOSTER SYNDROME AND WAYS WE COPE WITH ANGER AND FEAR

Imposter syndrome occurs when high achievers doubt their abilities and accomplishments. They can't believe they're successful and feel anxious or depressed, fearing they'll be exposed as frauds. The cycle includes perfectionism, trying too hard, fear of failure, denying competence, and avoiding success.[9]

Imposter syndrome was first noticed in 1978 among successful women and marginalized groups,[10] though I learned of it only a few years ago. The more I learned, the more I recognized the symptoms in my life. I'm convinced it all comes back to that ugly four-letter word: *fear*. In my career transition from engineer to homeschooler to writer, I have battled imposter syndrome. I'm constantly learning and not feeling like the supreme expert that I once was when I worked as an engineer, but the truth is, I *am* an expert in my niche as writer through lived experience, education, and research. Having to repeatedly convince myself of this fact is a tell-tale sign of some imposter syndrome going on. Take a look at the six characteristics of imposter syndrome.

1. Failure to internalize success
2. Perfectionism
3. Super-heroism
4. Atychiphobia (fear of failure)
5. Denial of competence and capability
6. Achievemephobia (fear of success)[11]

We've all believed at some point that we can have whatever we desire. Take the army's slogan "Be all that you can be" or the idea of the American dream. Yet, as Black women we are often met with setbacks. Some coping strategies Black women use include spiritual bypassing, emotional distancing, and quiet quitting.

I first heard of *spiritual bypassing* in 2022 when I was a guest on the podcast *Today's Heartlift with Janell*. The term was coined by psychologist and Buddhist practitioner John Welwood in 1984. Spiritual bypassing refers to when people use spiritual beliefs or practices to avoid dealing with their emotional problems. Instead of facing their issues, they focus on spiritual things to feel better. This might include ignoring negative feelings, being overly positive, or pretending to be more enlightened than they are. Spiritual bypassing can then lead to problems such as feeling disconnected from emotions, trying to control others, or having an addiction. It doesn't help in the long run because it stops true emotional healing from

happening.[12] We should strive to become healthy in all areas
of life physically, mentally, and spiritually. Spiritual bypassing
hinders that, because it's not healthy to overlook our pain.
Rather, we must acknowledge it and take it to God so he can
help heal it.

An example of what may lead to spiritual bypassing is the
use of a particular verse in Scripture to nudge you to "get
over" whatever is concerning you. Perhaps because of how
that verse has been used against you in the past, or maybe because you incorporate that verse into your self-talk, you end
up not giving yourself the grace to face some of the hard things
you're experiencing.

Emotional distancing is another coping strategy by which
people distance themselves from what is causing an unwanted
emotional response in an attempt to appear stronger than they
really are—even if it means, for example, walking out of a loved
one's wake or funeral.[13] This reminds me of some letters I found
within the last year or so that some of my family members wrote
to me when I was away at college. Among them were letters
from my dad and my sister Sharon, who are no longer on this
side of heaven. Though I was happy when I found them, I
knew I wasn't prepared to read them. So I bundled them up
and placed them on a bookshelf. I didn't try to kid myself: I
knew I was avoiding reading them. But I did allow myself the
time I needed to be ready to read them.

Lastly, *quiet quitting* is a strategy for dealing with prolonged
grief and pain when things seem as if they will never change.
When we are tired, we often move inward. I went through a

season of quiet quitting just before leaving corporate America. I had been overlooked for a promotion and was unable to move to any other department, even though I received high evaluations and was told that I was a valued employee. I was passionate about my work as a subject matter expert, but this experience was so discouraging that I truly started doing the bare minimum. During meetings I listened to what others said, but when I had an idea, I kept it to myself. I didn't realize I was doing this until a coworker began asking me why I wasn't talking much in the meetings. She noted, "You always have something to say." (I hope she meant in a good way and not in the angry-Black-woman way!)

The term *quiet quitting* has been defined and redefined many times over the past few years. In simple terms, it means not being mentally "there" at work. But the idea of quiet quitting can also be applied to how Black women cope in our world and culture. It is the way we survive—whether it's right, wrong, or simply the way it is.

NAVIGATING ANGER

Let's see what the Bible says about anger. Emotions are a natural part of the human experience. Anger is part of our well of emotions. Thus, anger in and of itself is not sinful. Paul wrote, "In your anger do not sin: do not let the sun go down while you are still angry" (Ephesians 4:26). Some ways we might sin in our anger include expressing violent rage through our actions, refusing to forgive, spreading slander and gossip, disrespecting authority, and hating our neighbor. This essentially means anything that is against the Word of God that does not show the fruit of the spirit and/or the nature of Christ.

In her book *Healing Racial Trauma*, Sheila Wise Rowe notes, "Most African Americans are unaware of the impact that pent-up pain can have. Rage is one result. Rage builds over time as a result of cumulative suppressed emotions precipitated by voicelessness."[14] Thinking about grief as perceived anger makes me think of Job's wife. Throughout the book of Job, she is unnamed and usually only referred to as his nagging wife. But I want us to take another look at her. Though unnamed, she no doubt has faced tremendous suffering. Every loss of Job's—his servants, his livestock, his children, and his health—is also her loss. She is grieving too, but she's only known as the complainer because of these words written about her.

After Job is plagued with a skin disease, his wife can no longer hold in her grief and says, "Are you still maintaining your integrity? Curse God and die!" (Job 2:9). Her heart is totally hardened. When we are grieving, we cannot think straight or see clearly. The story of Job's wife mostly serves as an example to women of how not to act, but it's also a reminder that we are human. We can relate to Job's wife on some level at some point in our lives. As Black women we endure many losses, and most often no one is extending us grace to grieve. Our outward expression of anger becomes a shield to protect us. As a result, our response to grief is often highlighted in a negative light by others. Our hearts harden and become calloused. Yet, God can turn any heart of stone into a heart of flesh (Ezekiel 36:26).

NAVIGATING FEAR

When it comes to fear as a secondary response to grief, I think of the many times God says, "Fear not," or "Do not be afraid" in the Bible. In fact, it's written 365 times. Anything repeated by God is important for us to heed. "Fear not, for I am with you; be not dismayed, for I am your God; I will strengthen you, I will help you, I will uphold you with my righteous right hand" (Isaiah 41:10 ESV). Most often the words proceed from angels, such as when the angel appeared to Mary, the mother of Jesus, and said, "Do not be afraid, Mary; you have found favor with God" (Luke 1:30).

In 2 Timothy, Paul writes to Timothy, his understudy, "For the Spirit God gave us does not make us timid, but gives us power, love and self-discipline" (2 Timothy 1:7). The context of Paul's words leading up to this verse is important, as we see some of Timothy's fears and ways to combat them.

- *The fear of going against the grain.* "As I urged you when I went into Macedonia, stay there in Ephesus so that you may command certain people not to teach false doctrines any longer or to devote themselves to myths and endless genealogies. Such things promote controversial speculations rather than advancing God's work—which is by faith. The goal of this command is love, which comes from a pure heart and a good conscience and a sincere faith" (1 Timothy 1:3-5). We can fear going against the grain because of the fear of judgment. We wonder if people will ask *Who does she think she is?* But the truth is, when we look at everyone who has made an impact on the kingdom of God, they went against the grain. But even more so, we see that God was with them, so there is nothing to fear.

- *The fear of ungodly leaders.* "I urge, then, first of all, that petitions, prayers, intercession, and thanksgiving be made for all people—for kings and all those in authority, that we may live peaceful and quiet lives in all godliness and holiness. This is good, and pleases God our Savior, who wants all people to be saved and to come to a knowledge of the truth" (1 Timothy 2:1-4). When we pray things change. Second Chronicles 7:14 says that if we pray, seek God's face, and turn from our wicked ways, he will forgive and heal our land. Thus, we are urged to pray and intercede for leaders. Including leadership of our country, our churches, our employers, and our households if applicable.

- *The fear of others' responses.* "If I am delayed, you will know how people ought to conduct themselves in God's household, which is the church of the living God, the pillar and foundation of the truth" (1 Timothy 3:15). Being discerning helps us understand the motives of those around us and helps us respond to our grief. Discernment can help us navigate different situations, as well as how we can better serve others.

- *The fear of unmet needs.* "Anyone who does not provide for their relatives, and especially for their own household, has denied the faith and is worse than an unbeliever"

(1 Timothy 5:8). There are so many people who have needs for various reasons, and we may fear that we cannot meet everyone's needs. And the truth is we can't, but God can. We may also fear our needs will go unmet. Yet, we can care for others in ways the Lord leads us to and trust God to meet all of our needs.

Things happen that cause us to fear. That's natural in the world we live in, especially for Black women. What is fear keeping you from?

A biblical solution for fear is to cast the whole of our care on Jesus because he cares for us. But what does that really look like day to day? Philippians 4:6-7 says, "Do not be anxious about anything, but in every situation, by prayer and petition, with thanksgiving, present your requests to God. And the peace of God, which transcends all understanding, will guard your hearts and your minds in Christ Jesus." Giving all of our cares and worries to God could look like writing them down in a journal or even in the notes app on our phone. It could be whispering a breath prayer to God. It could be listening to praise and worship music. It could be lamenting unto the Lord. It could be practicing gratitude.

Paul remembered Timothy's faith and urged him to fan the flame. May we live in such a way that others remember our faith, especially in these politically and racially charged times. May we reflect Jesus and be the reason someone still believes in him, calls on him, and hopes in him.

Dear Black woman,

There are inevitably times when we are fearful and angry—so fearful that we're breaking into a cold sweat, and so angry it feels as if the heat coming from our brow could fry an egg. We have every right to feel that way. Fear and anger are real. Sometimes they are heavy. But you know what? God living within us is bigger than anything that confronts us. With God, we can face these emotions instead of pushing them aside to let them fester or rule over our lives. We are free in Christ. God has equipped us with everything we need to navigate through the weeds of our emotions. We can bring them to him one by one, moment by moment as they come, casting our cares on him so that we can live the life he has called us to.

7

UNHINGED HEALING

Dear friend, I pray that you may enjoy good health
and that all may go well with you,
even as your soul is getting along well.

3 John 2

One night I received a call that a close friend was in the ER. I went to her as fast as I could. When I arrived, I learned she was there due to a suicide attempt. Though I was relieved she was still alive, I couldn't get past the gaping hole at her wrist held together by a few staples, and I fainted right then and there.

The next thing I knew, I awoke on the floor to a nurse's voice asking if I was okay. So many thoughts were running through my mind. For one, *Gross, I passed out on a dirty hospital floor.* Two, *Why had this happened? Didn't this Black woman know how much she was loved?* I couldn't wrap my mind around what had taken place. Even now I'm unclear about all the events that led to that particular night. I do know that it wasn't the first attempt. I was grateful she was still here, but also mad and sad that it had happened again.

She'd mentioned that "it" was all just too much—whatever *it* was. I wish I could have taken away her pain. Have you also felt fiercely helpless while seeing a loved one struggle? Watching her life from the sidelines and being tagged in only at certain times was hard. The trauma I witnessed in her life was crushing for all who were involved. It felt like she could never get a break. She loved hard. She had dreams. She was a first-generation college student. She experienced abuse from her partners and husbands. She was a single Black mom. She turned to alcohol for comfort as well as to God. Through it all, she just wanted healing.

Suicide is an all too familiar topic for Black women that isn't talked about often. As I write, there have been several cases highlighted in the media of prominent Black women who died by suicide.

Healing is messy. Though we may not always have the full story, we can agree that the challenges and trauma we face as Black women are compounded when we add raising children into the mix—whether they are biological, adopted, or our family or friend's kids. This means we are the village. Hustle culture doesn't help because it makes us believe that we have to be all things and do all things. And in turn, we don't take the time to rest and heal.

The American Psychological Association defines *trauma* as any disturbing experience that results in significant fear, help-lessness, dissociation, confusion, or other disruptive feelings intense enough to have a long-lasting negative effect on a person's attitudes, behavior, and other aspects of functioning.[1] According to research, trauma can change our behavior, our cognitive state, our emotions, and even our biochemistry. This may put someone in a state of chaos, which causes them to lose their sense of security.[2]

Awareness is key to healing in healthy ways. As the saying goes, we cannot heal what we do not name. It would be years before I came to know the effects that past trauma had on my life—how it informed the way I raised my kids, the men I chose, and my relationships with others. It affected every area, even my spiritual life. For a while, I couldn't trust church leaders. They didn't feel safe. This goes to show that trauma shakes our very core, affecting our decisions, our outlook on life, and our future.

When I was almost six years old, my family loaded up into my Aunt Glory's VW Beetle, not knowing we were in for a rude awakening. We went around a curve on Highway 17 like the famous racecar driver Dale Earnhardt, only we didn't stick the landing. When we rounded the curve, the car flipped and flipped again. Me, my sister Charlotte, my mom, my Aunt Emma, my grandma, and Aunt Glory went flying. Thankfully, we sustained only minor physical injuries, including a broken arm and a sprained arm and neck. God was good and gracious to us. Still, this experience has stuck with me, and not in the best of ways. While driving recently, I imagined going around the curve too fast and the same thing happening. I've also experienced this feeling with my daughter, who is a new driver. Then I catch myself in a panic and remember where it's coming from.

Research suggests that those who have been traumatized are either so alert to dangers around them that they can't enjoy life, they are too numb to be present, or they ignore signs of danger altogether.[3] Though trauma can manifest in various ways, there are particular indicators of trauma that we can be aware of in our lives. Here are some signs of emotional trauma in adults.

- Avoidance of people or places associated with the traumatic event
- Intrusive thoughts or memories about the event
- Nightmares or flashbacks about the event
- Intrusive feelings of guilt or shame
- Feeling "on edge" or easily startled
- Problems sleeping
- Difficulties concentrating
- Irritability or outbursts of anger

Sufferers of emotional trauma may also turn to alcohol or drugs to cope with their symptoms.[4]

Do any of these signs resonate with you? I've started keeping a running list. I completed an assessment several years ago that mapped out traumatic events in my life. So many of the events happened before I even entered my early twenties. I carried these traumas into adulthood and have only started processing them over the past four years or so.

Bessel van der Kolk writes in his book *The Body Keeps the Score*, "Nobody can 'treat' away abuse, rape, molestation, or any other horrendous event, for that matter; what has happened cannot be undone. But what can be dealt with are the imprints of the trauma on the body, mind, and soul . . . trauma robs you of the feeling that you are in charge of yourself."[5] Further, Van der Kolk says,

The challenge of recovery is to reestablish ownership of your body and your mind—of yourself. This means feeling free to know what you know and to feel what you feel without becoming overwhelmed, enraged, ashamed, or collapsed. For most people, this involves:

1. Finding a way to become calm and focused.

2. Learning to maintain that calm in response to images, thoughts, sounds, or physical sensations that remind you of the past.

3. Finding a way to be fully alive in the present and engaged with the people around you.

4. Not having to keep secrets from yourself including secrets about the ways you managed to survive.[6]

I love to tell the story of a counselor I was seeing. I'd grown keen on her, as my husband and I had seen her on and off for several years for marriage maintenance. (Side note: counseling as maintenance versus repair is the best thing.) Since we were familiar with each other already, I started doing individual counseling with her after I wrote my first book. After getting all my grief stories down on paper, everything brewed and rose to the surface—too much all at once. Though I have already experienced so much healing, I still have a long journey ahead.

We jumped into my grief timeline, starting from the beginning. After about three sessions, she asked if we could take a break because it was affecting her. I love this story because it affirms all the trauma I had been carrying for so long. It was a lot for anyone, even for someone who was listening to me talk about it. My trauma was too much for her; it's too much for me. But I'm grateful it's not too much for God. So if you find yourself exhibiting signs of emotional trauma, don't despair. You are not alone. I am with you, and God is with you. As you become more aware of the signs and triggers of trauma and grief, you will be better able to cope in day-to-day life.

As Black women, we may not even recognize the trauma we have experienced. Now, you might be saying, "Hold up, you're about to get all up in the Kool-Aid and don't even know the flavor." But part of healing is naming those things that inform the way we live and make decisions, even if we don't realize what they are. For me, it has been an unfolding of childhood trauma.

When I was seven years old, my dad had one of multiple blackout spells—at least, that's what my family called them. We never did figure out what caused them. I remember my mom calling, "The ambulance is here," followed by paramedics marching through the door with bags and gear in hand to assist my dad. They soon rushed back through the door and returned with a rolling bed to wheel him out to the ambulance. My mom rode in the back with him and told the rest of us, "Y'all stay here." Though these incidents happened so long ago, the sound of my dad falling to the floor with a thud, as if he were dead, stays with me and still wrecks my nerves to this day.

This is where posttraumatic stress disorder (PTSD) entered my story. I hate labeling things, but it does help to inform why we feel the way we feel, why we do the things we do, and what is happening inside us.

Most often when we think of PTSD, we think of it only affecting men and women who have served in the military and been affected by war. Yet, classic PTSD is defined by behaviors such as reliving a traumatic event, steering clear of anything that triggers unwanted memories, and increasing fresh reactions to the event.[7]

These days, when I hear a thud in our house while my kids are playing or walking around upstairs, my heart sinks to my stomach. I know everything is okay, but for a split second, I don't.

Research suggests that we're starting to see how intense experiences impact how we relate to our bodies and the world around us. Trauma isn't just something that happened in the past; it's also the mark it leaves on our minds, brains, and bodies. This mark affects how we cope with life now.[8] Recognizing how your body reacts to certain things is key to acknowledging and processing trauma. What has your body kept score of over the years that you may now be feeling physically?

Racial trauma is a particular form of trauma that may also leave a mark physically, emotionally, and mentally. Sheila Wise Rowe defines several forms of racial trauma:

- *Racial trauma*—the physical and psychological symptoms that people of color often experience after a stressful racist incident

- *Historical racial trauma*—shared by a group rather than an individual and spans multiple generations who carry trauma-related symptoms without having been present for the past traumatizing event
- *Transgenerational racial trauma*—the specific experience of trauma across a specific family line
- *Personal racial trauma*—trauma someone has personally experienced
- *Physical trauma*—trauma experienced physically to someone's body
- *Vicarious trauma*—trauma experienced after someone hears detailed trauma stories or watches videos of what the deceased or survivors endured in a traumatic event
- *Microaggressions*—little by little discriminations that add up
- *Racial gaslighting*—ways individuals or institutions try to manipulate or question people of color's sense of reality, often to assert or maintain control, superiority, or power[9]

Toni Morrison's novel *Beloved* is inspired by the true story of Margaret Garner, a slave who murdered her daughter with her own hands so she could escape slavery through death. Garner was later driven to madness.[10] Her story is traumatic and disturbing—yet it forces us to recognize the brutality of what it meant to endure the trauma of slavery and its conditions.

Though our experiences are not the same as Garner's, we still carry trauma. So what do we do with it?

THREE STAGES OF RECOVERY FROM TRAUMA

Judith Herman, an American psychiatrist and trauma expert known for her work in the area of trauma psychology, researched and outlined a way of understanding trauma by creating the three stages of recovery from trauma.

Stage one: Establishment of safety. This stage involves creating a secure and stable environment for the survivor, both physically and emotionally. It includes ensuring the individual's physical safety from further harm and providing a supportive and validating space where they feel heard and understood. This stage is crucial for building trust and rapport between the survivor and their support system, as well as laying the foundation for further healing and recovery from trauma.

Stage two: Remembrance and mourning. During this stage, individuals confront and process their traumatic experiences, allowing themselves to remember and acknowledge what happened to them. This involves exploring the memories, emotions, and thoughts associated with the trauma in a safe and supportive environment. Through therapy, storytelling, journaling, or other forms of expression, survivors begin to make sense of their experiences and grieve the losses they have endured. This stage is essential for integrating the fragmented pieces of the trauma narrative and reclaiming a sense of agency and control over their life. By honoring their pain and mourning their losses, survivors can begin to release the emotional burdens of the past and move toward healing and recovery.

Stage three: Reconnection. During this stage, individuals focus on rebuilding their sense of connection with themselves,

others, and the world around them. This involves reestab-
lishing trust in relationships, cultivating a sense of safety and
belonging, and rediscovering a sense of purpose and meaning
in life. Survivors may engage in activities that promote self-care,
self-expression, and personal growth, such as therapy, support
groups, creative outlets, and spiritual practices. By nurturing
healthy relationships, pursuing meaningful goals, and engaging
in activities that bring joy and fulfillment, survivors gradually
reintegrate into society and reclaim a sense of wholeness and
vitality. This stage is essential for promoting long-term healing
and resilience after trauma.[11]

For Black women, these stages of recovery show the importance of feeling safe, remembering and grieving past traumas,
and reconnecting with ourselves and our communities. Safety
means finding places where we feel protected both physically
and emotionally, such as supportive networks and culturally
sensitive mental health services. When dealing with past
traumas, we may need to talk about and honor those experiences, finding comfort in our cultural heritage and support
from our communities. Reconnecting means rebuilding relationships and finding strength in our identity and shared experiences. This approach to healing recognizes the challenges
we face and emphasizes the power of support and connection
in overcoming them.

THREE STEPS OF HEALTHY PROCESSING OF TRAUMA

In the remembrance and mourning stage of recovery, individuals confront and process their traumatic experiences,

allowing themselves to remember and acknowledge what happened to them. This stage of the recovery process can be broken down further into three steps for healthy processing. ***Step one: Experiencing the event.*** During this step, the person undergoes intense emotional and physical reactions as they directly face the threatening or harmful situation. This may include feelings of fear, helplessness, or horror as well as physiological responses such as increased heart rate, sweating, or trembling. The experience of the event can be overwhelming and disorienting, and the individual may struggle to make sense of what is happening in the moment. This is a critical stage in the trauma processing journey, as it lays the foundation for how the individual will perceive, process, and respond to the traumatic experience in the subsequent stages of healing and recovery.

Step two: Mourning. This step involves acknowledging and processing the emotional pain and loss associated with the traumatic event. During this step, individuals allow themselves to grieve the losses they have experienced as a result of the trauma, including loss of safety, trust, control, and innocence. This process may involve expressing emotions such as sadness, anger, guilt, or shame, as well as confronting painful memories and feelings associated with the trauma. Through mourning, individuals begin to make meaning of their experiences and integrate them into their personal narratives. It is a necessary step in the healing journey, as it allows individuals to honor their emotions, validate their experiences, and gradually release the emotional burden of the trauma, paving the way for further healing and growth.

Step three: Integrating the experience. This is the final phase where individuals work toward incorporating their traumatic experiences into their overall sense of self and life story. During this step, individuals seek to make sense of their experiences, reconcile conflicting emotions and beliefs, and find a new sense of coherence and meaning in their lives. This process involves integrating the lessons learned from the trauma into their personal narrative, acknowledging how it has shaped their identity, beliefs, and relationships. Through integration, individuals strive to move beyond the trauma and reclaim a sense of agency, purpose, and resilience. It is a transformative journey of self-discovery and growth, as individuals learn to embrace their past experiences as part of their journey toward healing and wholeness.[12]

As Black women, trauma often involves confronting intersecting challenges of systemic racism, gender-based violence, and socioeconomic disparities, which leads to intense emotional and physical reactions. These steps allow us to mourn the collective traumas of our communities and ancestors as well as to integrate our traumatic experiences into our sense of self and identity, drawing on cultural practices, community support, and spiritual resilience to forge a path toward healing and liberation. This demonstrates the importance of acknowledging Black women's pain, honoring our resilience, and reclaiming our power in the face of adversity.

I encourage you to use these stages and steps to recovery to inform your processing and navigation through trauma rather than view them as rules that must be followed linearly. Pain, suffering, and destruction are healthy reactions to trauma, allowing us to wrestle with the traumatic events so we can process and integrate them. In healthy processing, a traumatic event transforms and integrates into our personality, restoring emotional balance.

However, because we are carriers of our experiences, various traits, habits, and challenges can be passed along generationally if they are not dealt with appropriately. Especially vulnerable are children who grow up in societies that have experienced trauma. These child survivors often struggle because even their good relationships with their parents can be affected. When a parent is dealing with their own fears and stresses, they might not be able to comfort their child properly. This can lead to children feeling insecure and learning to comfort themselves. For children born during times of widespread trauma, feeling safe and trusting others doesn't come naturally. They then pass this lack of trust down to their own kids in the next generation.[13]

THE STORY OF TAMAR

Genesis 38 introduces us to Tamar, an ancestor of the infamous King David and the daughter-in-law of Judah, one of Joseph's brothers. When Tamar's husband Er dies, she marries his brother. After her second husband also dies, she is pushed to the side as a childless widow of no value. After a long time, she disguises herself and conceives a child with her father-in-law, Judah, in order to bear a child in the family line of her husband Er.

Tamar's story is strange, and she is often misunderstood because she comes across as manipulative. But in reality, she was being mishandled by the men in her life, as she was lied to repeatedly, sexually abused, and denied her rights. Instead of succumbing to a life of being thrown to the side, she took matters into her own hands.

To be clear, I don't think Tamar's story encourages us to take things into our own hands. Rather, we see time and time again in the Bible that God is in control and wants us to be led by the Holy Spirit in the way we should go. Nevertheless, Tamar's story is important. It shows that even during biblical times, women were treated in horrendous ways. I wish I could go back in time to tell her, "It's not your fault what happened to you." Sometimes the first step toward healing is acknowledging that what happened to us is not our fault.

Tamar shows up in Jesus' lineage in Matthew 1:3. What does that signify, and what does it mean for Black women today who have been used and abused?

Tamar's significant place in history shows God's care for the overlooked and marginalized. She foreshadows Jesus' ministry to those deemed unlikely to be chosen by God. Tamar's story helps us as Black women feel seen, heard, and understood. I believe everything we experience is represented in some way in God's Word, as if he is saying, "I see you. I'm here." Tamar's story also bears witness to traumas faced by many Black women, including being silenced for experiencing a trauma, carrying a succession of losses, and being a victim of abuse, whether sexual, mental, or physical.

These are topics that often go unspoken in our churches, leaving Black women to navigate these struggles alone. I want to pause to make space for you. If you are having a challenging time and need to speak with someone, you can call 988 to connect with the National Suicide Prevention Lifeline (https://988lifeline.org). Trained crisis counselors are available at any moment, whether for thoughts of suicide, a mental health or substance use crisis, or other emotional help.

Dear Black woman,

What happened to you was not your fault. There have been times when I felt what happened to me was my fault—like if I hadn't done x, y, or z, it would not have happened. Sure, sometimes we act foolishly and have to reap the consequences. But I'm talking about things that were truly not our fault—things that we often keep to ourselves, things that many women have even taken to the grave. This is to encourage you that the God who sees everything sees you. He has not turned a blind eye to your pain and suffering. God knows you. God understands.

8

REST AS RESISTANCE

Each person deserves a day away in which no problems are
confronted, no solutions searched for. Each of us needs to
withdraw from the cares which will not withdraw from us.

DR. MAYA ANGELOU

DURING MY COLLEGE YEARS, I held down three jobs while being a full-time engineering student. Why, you may ask? You would think I needed those jobs to pay for essentials like books, housing, and food, but I really just wanted the money for going out, taking epic spring break trips, getting my hair done, and buying cool clothes. Now that I think about it, I was probably more high maintenance in college than I am right now. I guess that's what marriage and kids will do to you.

But seriously, I mention this because if we fast forward fifteen years, slowing down is still a challenge for me. Peace Amadi, a friend who works within the mental health space, posted this on social media: "Being unable to rest is a trauma response. What happened to make you so afraid of rest?" These words stopped me in my tracks, and I began to ask myself that question. I realized that all the loss I'd experienced starting in my teen years was catching up with me because I had not processed it.

So if you find yourself "too busy" for rest, self-care, and soul care, dear Black woman, what happened to make you so afraid of rest?

I'm just going to let that sit there as I continue.

OUR BODIES NEED REST

Dr. Saundra Dalton-Smith, author of *Sacred Rest*, shares about the different types of rest we need, which include physical, mental, emotional, sensory, creative, social, and spiritual. Though various types of rest are mentioned here, research suggests Black women view rest as more of a physical act.[1]

What is the first thing that comes to mind when you think about needing to rest? Maybe you ask yourself how much sleep you got the night before. After all, sleep health influences every facet of human function and is essential for helping with cardiovascular, immune, brain, and mental health.[2] Research also suggests Black Americans are more likely than white Americans to sleep fewer than six hours each night, suffer from sleep apnea, suffer from insomnia, and are more likely to suffer from excessive daytime sleepiness.[3] I can think of friends, family members, and others I know, including myself, who suffer from one or more of these. And there are so many reasons why a Black woman might be lacking in sleep.

Yet, given what we know, we need more than a nap when our soul is tired.

We as Black women find rest to be one of the hardest things to come by. Yet, biblically speaking, rest is the resistance to trauma. Matthew 11:28-30 says, "Come to me, all you who are weary and burdened, and I will give you rest. Take my yoke upon you and learn from me, for I am gentle and humble in heart, and you will find rest for your souls. For my yoke is easy and my burden is light." What's more, God set an example for us by resting after six days of work: "The Sabbath was made for man, not man for the Sabbath" (Mark 2:27). God blessed the Sabbath day, signifying that rest is not only needed, but it is also holy. Additionally, Saundra Dalton-Smith writes that refusing to rest strips us of everything that is holy.[4] That is a powerful revelation.

SABBATH REST

I spoke on the topic of rest at a conference several years ago, which was quite ironic because I struggle with rest. Still, it was an amazing opportunity to seek God and his Word to center my heart on rest, as my soul and body desperately needed it.

The Sabbath is a day of religious observation and abstinence from work. Sabbath comes from the Hebrew word *shavat*, meaning "to cease or rest." It is kept by Jews from Friday evening to Saturday evening and by most Christians on Sunday.

I grew up learning about the Sabbath from my mom, who took it to mean "no work." On Sundays we couldn't clean, iron, cook, cut grass, nothing. She would iron our clothes the night before and also cook the night before and warm up the food after church, so that we did what she considered to be no work on Sundays.

I thought this was a bit much at first, but I learned Mom had the right idea. I wondered, though, if someone who was required to work on Sundays was sinning against God. As I got older, I learned the answer was no—the practice of sabbath can look different for each of us. It doesn't necessarily have to refer to Sunday or Saturday; it simply means "a time of rest."

One thing I'm beginning to realize is that rest is holy work. When we don't take the time to rest, we hinder our souls from prospering. I think about all the prep work that goes into family vacations. Sometimes the planning of it all can be so exhausting that I start to think it might be better to just stay home. But once we get everything packed, hit the road, and reach our destination, it's all worth it. So yes, it takes *work* to rest.

If you are like me, you're busy with all the things with not enough time to catch your breath, and you wish you could add more time to the day, the week, or the month. (Or better yet, could every day just be Saturday? Saturdays with coffee and Jesus sound like a great place to live in.) But I believe God wants us to live in such a way that we are not always wishing for the weekend. Though this may seem unrealistic at times, believing that it's not possible to live a life that includes rest is a lie from Satan who would love for us to work ourselves to the bone until we become of no use to anyone, especially to God.

God wants our entire being healed and whole. Third John 2 (KJV) says, "Beloved, I wish above all things that thou mayest prosper and be in health, even as thy soul prospereth." What's more, 1 Peter 2:24 proclaims, "'He himself bore our sins' in his body on the cross, so that we might die to sins and live for righteousness; 'by his wounds you have been healed.'"

These verses tell us that loving God and resting in God are good for our soul. And it starts with the idea of slowing down. We might not even comprehend the concept of *slow* anymore because of our cultural influences. We are a fast-paced, need-to-know-everything society as we try to keep up with everything going on around us through the news and social media. But God didn't create us with the capacity to go, go, go and never stop. Instead, he created us with the need to rest and replenish our souls. The best part is, he made provision for us to do so through the Sabbath. Praise be to God, who never leaves us without a plan and gives an answer for everything we need.

THE HOLY WORK OF REST

These days you might hear someone say, "I'm taking a short sabbatical from Facebook." While that's all well and good, it's helpful to go deeper than social media. Let me start at the very beginning.

During the creation of the world, God included a day of rest. He created the heavens and the earth in six days, "and on the seventh day God ended His work which He had done, and He rested on the seventh day from all His work which He had done. Then God blessed the seventh day and sanctified it, because in it He rested from all His work which God had created and made" (Genesis 2:2-3 NKJV). I love to look at the Bible knowing that what's important to God should also be important to us.

Let's take a look at the Ten Commandments. The fourth commandment addresses soul care: "Remember the sabbath day, to keep it holy" (Exodus 20:8 KJV). Remember how my mom's rule of not doing anything on Sundays seemed like overkill at the time? Some people believe the Ten Commandments are overkill or irrelevant because we no longer live under the law. Paul wrote, "For sin shall no longer be your master, because you are not under the law, but under grace" (Romans 6:14). Just think about the commandments to not kill or steal—they are no longer part of the law, but they still reflect wise and moral values that should be carried out as part of our earthly laws.

In his book *Emotionally Healthy Spirituality*, Peter Scazzero describes how we can read all the books and have all the tools for rest, yet we never get around to implementing any of it, and "if we aren't busy, we feel guilty that we waste time and are not productive."[5] Feeling guilty about resting—that's all me. And maybe it's you, too. The idea of rest and finding what is good for our soul feels a little hopeless at times.

But the truth is, rest isn't a *nice* to have—it's a *need* to have. Rest is holy work, but rest takes work. I have personally had to shift my mindset on this. In perceiving rest as self-care, I sometimes can't help but think of it as optional. For example, I'll only schedule a spa day if I happen to have time for it. I still haven't used the spa gift card from my husband from last Valentine's Day, even though I know I need it. Why do we do this to ourselves?

Instead of viewing rest as self-care, perhaps we should view it as soul care. Let's look at it as something ordained by God himself, which we need to live the life God intended for us. Richard Swenson writes in his book *Margin*, "It is God the Creator who made limits, and it is the same God who placed them within us for our protection."[6] God does not require us to go on like the Energizer Bunny to prove ourselves to him or to anyone else.

This goes back to what I mentioned earlier about busyness being a trauma response. Somehow, we've taught ourselves that busyness and lack of rest are honorable. But the truth is, adhering to God's design for rest will feed our spirit and in turn produce more fruit of the Spirit in our lives. Rest and soul care take an act of faith. The Bible says there is rest for the children of God:

> There remains, then, a Sabbath-rest for the people of God; for anyone who enters God's rest also rests from their works, just as God did from his. Let us, therefore, make every effort to enter that rest, so that no one will perish by following their example of disobedience. For the word of God is alive and active. Sharper than any double-edged sword, it penetrates even to dividing soul and spirit, joints and marrow; it judges the thoughts and attitudes of the heart. (Hebrews 4:9-12)

It's not just about taking the time to rest but also about what you do with that time. Have you ever taken a vacation and found yourself to be just as tired as before you left? I personally have experienced this both before and after kids. I have also thought about implementing a sabbatical concept in my home-school schedule, which involves taking every seventh week off, but never have. Unfortunately, it often takes a burnout, a breakdown, or even a pandemic shutdown for us to understand that what we really need is rest for our souls.

WHAT THE BIBLE HAS TO SAY ABOUT REST

The story of Mary and Martha demonstrates the importance of rest. When Jesus came to their house, Martha—being the excellent host she was—started cleaning and preparing all the things. (If she was like me, she did most of her housework when expecting guests.) Yet, Martha got a slap on the wrist for this.

Meanwhile, Mary—instead of allowing herself to become busy—chose to sit at the feet of Jesus. Jesus uses Mary as an example for the disciples and all of us saying, "Mary has chosen what is better, and it will not be taken away from her" (Luke 10:42). Resting in Jesus will always be better than busying ourselves with the things of this world. By resting in him and at his feet, we then gain the strength to do other things we need to do.

In another example of rest, Jesus was with his apostles: "Then, because so many people were coming and going that they did not even have a chance to eat, he said to them, 'Come with me by yourselves to a quiet place and get some rest'" (Mark 6:31). We find Jesus going away to a quiet place often throughout the New Testament, showing us the significance of this practice for our lives as well.

You may be thinking, *Isn't the Sabbath more of a religious thing?* I submit to you that it's a God thing. Sabbath rest isn't a religious chore but a gift from God to his children to help us live our best life. And as I mentioned earlier, God, in creating us, knew we would need rest for our souls and thus made provision for us by way of the Sabbath. Mark wrote, "The Sabbath was made to meet the needs of people, and not people to meet the requirements of the Sabbath" (Mark 2:27 NLT).

So what do we gain from a life of observing the Sabbath and practicing times of rest? Psalm 92:12-14 declares that we are planted, we grow, we flourish, we bear fruit, and we stay healthy and strong. Isaiah 58:13-14 says we find joy in the Lord by honoring the Sabbath. These verses suggest that through rest we will have joy. When we keep the Sabbath we are delighting ourselves in the Lord, and in so doing, he gives us the desires of our hearts (Psalm 37:4). We are also reminded of these familiar words from the psalmist: "He makes me lie down in green pastures, he leads me beside quiet waters, he refreshes my soul. He guides me along the right paths for his name's sake" (Psalm 23:2-3).

STILL NOT CONVINCED?

If you're still not convinced and need some definitive reasons to rest, here are three:

1. A sabbath gives God the opportunity to provide for us supernaturally. When we tithe 10 percent of our income to God, he takes care of the remaining 90 percent. Similarly, if we commit to a sabbath, God will bless the remainder of our time.

2. A sabbath allows us to rest and be refreshed. Exodus 31:17 says, "It will be a sign between me and the Israelites forever, for in six days the LORD made the heavens and the earth, and on the seventh day he rested and was refreshed."

3. There are consequences when we don't rest. If babies don't get enough rest, they become difficult to soothe and get tired, whiny, and cranky. The same happens when we don't get enough rest. It leaks out into our day-to-day life, and we become short-tempered, we lack patience, we get snappy, we have bad attitudes, etc. It's not that we are bad people; we simply have neglected a sabbath to rest and refresh ourselves.

God can heal instantaneously, but we must take action as well to promote healing, which includes taking time to rest. Sometimes it seems impossible. And sometimes it feels easier and is even comforting to hold on to the pain, as if it's become a part of us. But the implications of how it could affect generations to come if not dealt with are too great. Because whatever has happened to us informs our decisions, how we view life, and how we do life.

Dear Black woman,

Don't believe the lie that you cannot take time to rest. Don't believe the hype that you must go, go, go to achieve your dream or to be successful. Don't allow this world to pressure you into thinking there is always something that must be done and that you are the only one who can do it. Because this is not the case. There is a time and season for everything under the sun. Thus, there is a time for you to rest. God has made a way for you to escape the hustle and bustle of life to rest mentally, physically, and spiritually in him. He creates space for us to be still and know he is God. He gives us space to hide underneath his shadow and to lie beside still waters, and the authority to speak to the chaos around us, "Peace be still."

9

THE SOFTER LIFE

*Struggle is a never-ending process. Freedom is never really
won, you earn it and win it in every generation.*

CORETTA SCOTT KING

"I HATE TO USE THESE WORDS, but they said you were
overqualified," the human resources rep told me over the
phone. Earlier that week, after I had applied for an engineering
position, I'd sat on one side of a boardroom-style table as a
group of all-white male engineers grilled me. This wasn't new
to me—I had gone through the same thing during my college
years and throughout my career. Yet I couldn't remember ever
feeling more othered than in that moment. There was one man
in particular who seemed infuriated that I knew all the answers.
Instead of being overqualified, it seemed like I was just "over-
Black," and a woman at that.

Having been the subject matter expert in my field for seven
years at the time, I thought I had that job in the bag. After
nailing the roundtable firing squad interview, I sat with the

director of the department. We chatted about how we shared the same alma mater and were both engineering grads. *This job is mine,* I thought.

Big fat nope. It was too good to be true.

This is only one example of how I found myself in a sea of white males and navigating predominantly white spaces during my time in corporate America. These kinds of issues often sound political, but they simply address basic human rights.

Before my first promotion from engineering technician to engineer, I'd shared an office with a white guy who would tell it like it is. Whenever I was passed up for open engineer positions, he would tell me, "It's the good ole boy system, and you ain't in it," or "Oh, you know you're not in the pecking order."

He got on my last nerve, but I knew he was telling the truth. I just hated to believe it.

I eventually got that promotion. Several years later, I noticed colleagues around me were getting promoted to senior-level engineers. We were all doing the same work, so why wasn't I getting promoted? It was insane, the hoops I had to jump through to get that title. It made me so angry. I changed jobs and was met with similar challenges. Other employees were coming into the site at a higher level than I but with less experience. So when I saw an open position that would mean a promotion, I applied. I remember the day my boss called me into her office.

"You can't apply for a promotion. You'll never get it," she said.

"I'm well qualified," I responded.

She followed with, "Yeah, but you're needed here, so they won't move you. They've already told me."

I was thankful for her candor, though I was also angry. Yet in these scenarios, what I've found to be true, and may be true for you as well, is that more than being angry, I was deeply hurting. According to the "Women in the Workplace" 2023 survey, women of color are underrepresented, rarely promoted to manager, frequently face discrimination, and receive less support.[1] It is also a given that we have to work almost two or three times as hard to even be considered for a higher position.

We find ourselves under the constant pressure of the idea that we have to go big or go home, try harder, do more, don't stop until you reach the top, carry all the weight, never let them see you sweat. And it has to change.

STRESS AND COPING MODELS

Stress is defined as a state of mental or emotional strain or tension resulting from adverse or very demanding circumstances.[2] According to a 2022 study on gender and race-related stress among Black women, the top three stressors were safety of children, raising Black children and being the head of the family, and finances.[3] For me, stressors include anything that adds to my mental load. Reflecting on the topics we have already covered, we can all agree we have either been under a lot of stress, are currently under it, or will be in the future. Thus, these conversations are important for helping us become more aware of our stressors, ways to combat them, and practical tools we can implement to stay sane.

Pearlin's model, developed by renowned sociologist Leonard I. Pearlin, "distinguishes between three elements of stress: sources (e.g., life events, chronic stressors), outcomes (e.g., mental and physical health problems), and mediators (e.g., self-concepts, social support, coping skills)."[4] Pearlin's model outlines four stages of stress.[5]

1. A demand (which can be physical, psychological, or cognitive)

2. Appraisal of the demand and of the available resources and capability to deal with the demand

3. A negative response to the cognitive appraisal of the demand and the resources with various levels of cognitive and somatic anxiety, depression, fear, and anger

4. The stress response, which affects behavior and/or performance[6]

Take a minute to write down your current stressors. Are they work-related? Time-related? Mental? Physical? This is an opportunity to slow down and tend to your mind, body, and soul.

HUSTLE CULTURE MEETS THE SOFTER LIFE

Hustle culture seems to be part of our DNA. We often go and go until we can't go anymore. Yet, one way to combat hustle culture is to embrace a softer life. Nicole Jenkins, an assistant professor of sociology at Howard University, describes the soft life as "the journey of prioritizing self needs unapologetically."[7] In what ways is it different from self-care, soul care, or simple rest? The softer life is a lifestyle that revolves around slowing down. Creator and businesswoman Kimora Brown further clarifies that soft living "is about denouncing hustle culture, it's not about luxury culture."[8]

Just like the strong Black woman, however, Black women who hustle are praised. We are known for being able to take care of ourselves, even if it means working three jobs and running on fumes and five-hour energy drinks. I can't even begin to imagine what it would look like to slow down or to live a softer life. Black women like me struggle with this concept because we don't want to appear lazy.

I'm constantly being told, "You better slow down before you run yourself into the ground. You need to get somewhere and sit down." When I came across this idea of a softer life floating around the internet, I decided to take a deeper dive into it. I started reading my friend Jodi Grubb's book, *Live Slowly*, which has taught me that a softer life means a slower life. I love the words she uses to describe the concept of slow in the opening pages of her book:

S = shift: not an abrupt stop, but a slowing down like gears on a bike; a pivot

L = linger: this is a call to pause, take your time, and be present

O = open hands: expectant and yet vulnerable; asking God

W = watchful: observe; being alert in watching out for that pull back to hurry.[9]

A softer life can help us to manage our stressors better, process challenges, and make space for God and others. In what ways have you tried to cope with your stress?

THE SOFTER LIFE IN THE KINGDOM OF GOD

When we make space for God, we understand more about the kingdom of God, and we understand what he intended for our lives on this earth. The Garden of Eden, for example, clues us into the life God planned for us, and it was not hustle culture. Further, Scripture that teaches us about the kingdom of God helps us view our lives in more of a divine context as we live here on earth.

When I think about the kingdom of God, it reminds me of how we are living in the now and the not yet. God has all power and authority over all things right now. He is Alpha and Omega right now, knowing the end from the beginning. Yet, we are walking out the full picture of the plan he already created before the beginning of time. The kingdom of God is in process and in progress.[10]

God's kingdom principles bring heaven to earth every time. Having a kingdom mindset helps us to keep our focus in everything we do. This is easier said than done, however, especially when navigating loss and grief, because having a kingdom mindset looks and sounds like the total opposite of how our culture operates. Yet, as Ephesians 2:6 says, we have been raised with Christ and are seated in heavenly places. We don't have to wait to get to heaven to experience God's best, even in our grief, for we are reminded of these kingdom principles:

God turns our mourning to joy, God creates beauty from ashes, the last will be first, and those who humble themselves will be lifted up. Following these principles allows us to live above challenging circumstances such as loss because we operate with a kingdom attitude.

Here's the thing: we will always have boxes to check. There will always be times when we are treated unfairly. But when we continue to pour Jesus into every situation and circumstance we experience, we begin to bring heaven to earth.

EMBRACING SUFFERING

Viewing life through the lens of eternity is challenging when so much hardship stares us in the face. The world is misled by Satan, which means we can expect our systems to be broken. This is not to say we don't pray for things to get better, but we do acknowledge the why behind the broken systems. We were not meant to rely on them forever.

If we consider our earthly systems from a biblical perspective, we recognize that Satan has limited authority on the earth. Satan started in heaven but was then cast out: "How you have fallen from heaven, morning star, son of the dawn! You have been cast down to the earth, you who once laid low the nations!" (Isaiah 14:12). Similarly, some of our world systems may have started with good intentions, yet because the heart of man is wicked above all else, they began to get worse.

I haven't forgotten where I've come from. And though I'm changing the narrative for my children, that doesn't mean I can't advocate for those who still find themselves relying on broken systems.

In their book *The Fellowship of Suffering*, authors Paul Borthwick and Dave Ripper write, "Suffering comes with the territory." They continue,

> Semrad taught us that most human suffering is related to love and loss and that the job of therapists is to help people "acknowledge, experience, and bear" the reality of life—with all its pleasure and heartbreak. "The greatest sources of our suffering are the lies we tell ourselves," he'd say, urging us to be honest with ourselves about every facet of our experience. He often said that people can never get better without knowing what they know and feeling what they feel.[11]

I am a proponent of acknowledging emotions rather than stuffing away pain, hurt, loss, and suffering, because acknowledgment is where the healing begins. To address broken systems is to address this broken world. The *Fellowship of Suffering* suggests that if we assume an offensive rather than a defensive position, we have opportunities to seek out ways we can actively support and spur change. While this can feel overwhelming, nothing is too much for our God. We're not meant to save the world, but we know the One who does save.

At the same time, embracing that suffering comes with the territory may soften the blow. It's hard to fathom that there may never be a resolution to the problems, challenges, heartbreak, and grief we experience as Black women here on earth. But have you ever thought maybe we aren't supposed to? That the suffering and grief we experience associated with broken systems is simply part of being a Black woman? It's such a sobering thought. Yet, it makes the hope of heaven that much grander.

To live in a world where people who look like us are still oppressed, still wrongly accused, and still being judged by our skin . . . that's suffering. For Black women, the weight of mothering, caretaking, appointment setting, and so many other things fall on our shoulders. The mental load can feel unbearable. We must take life as it comes, moment by moment. When we're busy taking care of others, who takes care of us?

The answer is God.

Luke wrote, "And when he was demanded of the Pharisees, when the kingdom of God should come, he answered them and said, The kingdom of God cometh not with observation: Neither shall they say, Lo here! or, lo there! for, behold, the kingdom of God is within you" (Luke 17:20-21 KJV).

Dear Black woman,

Take a deep breath. The pressure to perform and constantly do more is real. It is beyond exhausting. Even as you read this, you may be stressed about being stressed. Remember the Word of the Lord, which tells us there is a rest for the people of God (Hebrews 4:9). We don't have to live by the world's expectations of us or even the expectations we place on ourselves that push us to run ourselves into the ground. Instead, may we be kingdom-minded and allow ourselves the space to rest in God. Let us live a God-breathed life in which we prosper as our soul prospers—and not necessarily monetarily but primarily in peace, love, and sound mind and body. May the Lord bless you and keep you now and always.

10

HOPE MATTERS

Love recognizes no barriers. It jumps hurdles, leaps fences,
penetrates walls to arrive at its destination full of hope.

DR. MAYA ANGELOU

Without hope, we would be lost, yet Jesus is our hope.

CHRISTIAN SMITH, MY TWELVE-YEAR-OLD SON

I'VE ALWAYS HOPED for better medical care for my family.
Half of my immediate family members died of complications
associated with cancer. Each time they received a fatal diag-
nosis, the words that followed were, "There's nothing else
we can do." In the back of my mind, I often thought, *Is that
the truth?* I'm sure this vein of thinking gets the better of us
no matter the color of our skin. But I know there is a track
record of Black people receiving less than the best treatment
in the medical system. Our family doesn't trust the staff to be
alone with the patient. That's why whenever one of my family

members is admitted to the hospital, at least one other family
member will undoubtedly be with them at all times. When
you witness things with your own eyes that you can't explain,
you start to put in more safeguards to provide some peace of
mind about the situation. That's what my mom and her family
have done and continue to do—because they hope for better
medical care.

Growing up, I had hoped for a better relationship between
my mom and dad. I remember the night my parents argued
and my dad slapped my mom midsentence. He'd never hit her
before and never did again. Knowing how feisty Mom is, I was
sure she would knock him to the ground. But she didn't. Instead, she turned, went into the bedroom, and started packing.
Though she didn't leave, Dad left our house and didn't come
back for months. I couldn't stop crying. I just couldn't believe
what had happened before my eyes.

At no more than eight years old, my heart broke for my
parents' marriage. I didn't know what this meant for me and
my sister Charlotte, who was still living at home. Mom kept
saying, "Y'all will never have another momma like me." That
hit hard because she made it sound like what happened was our
fault somehow. It made me think she wouldn't be there for us.
And it scared me. Looking back, though, I can see how being a
Black woman just took its toll on Momma.

Dad moved a few states away to find a better job to support
us, or so we were told. But it was really because my parents
were separated. He would send home money and sometimes
come back to visit my sisters and me. I was so young at the time

I didn't understand what was going on. I imagine now he just wanted a better life for himself and for us.

I was so happy when he came back home. He and my mom seemed to have worked out whatever issues they were having. Years later, I asked my mom what happened for my dad to come back during that time, though I dared not ask what caused him to leave. She said she wrote him a letter and told him to come home or else. I laughed out loud, thinking, *Black woman, you are powerful!* I imagine she put many other things in that letter that would probably make me blush.

In the end, before Dad died, he made amends. During one of his last visits to the hospital, Mom spent the night with him. He'd just had a port installed earlier in the day for chemotherapy treatment and received his first dose. The next morning when I arrived, he was all chatty and giddy. Before I could even step all the way into the room, he said, "Me and your mom had a good talk last night."

"You did?"

"Yeah, I told her I was sorry for everything I put her through."

All I could do was smile, hold back tears, and say, "That's so good, Daddy." My heart ached because I knew he knew his life was ending.

Over the years, I've hoped for many things. As Black women, we hope for many things. A better life for our family than the one we grew up in. Security and safety for our family and ourselves. A better education and career opportunities. Fair treatment. Representation. Strong community. A good life. Hope to not suffer injustices, to not bear the emotional weight of violence, nor to succumb to the statistics of early death. Sometimes it feels as if we can only hope.

HOPE THROUGH SPIRITUALS

The hope of Black women has always been rooted in faith, which we find in accounts of slavery. I think of negro spirituals, songs to help slaves endure day-to-day hardships by keeping their minds focused on Jesus and the hope of freedom. Some examples are "Steal Away to Jesus" and "Swing Low, Sweet Chariot." These spirituals were more than simply songs—they gave slaves hope on their road to freedom. Spirituals focused on enduring earthly sufferings in exchange for heavenly rewards, trusting God to right the wrongs done to them, as they provided emotional support in the midst of living in a world that lacked stability or safety.[1]

If you've ever had the privilege of being part of a gospel choir, you sang some of those spirituals. I started in the choir singing soprano. (Today you will find me singing comfortably in my alto range. I once heard Tye Tribbett at a concert say, "Altos are just lazy sopranos." That's about right, I'll take it.) But spirituals—what we call gospel songs today—continue to speak to the trials of everyday life. A few that come to mind are "I'm So Glad," "Trouble Don't Last Always," "Rough Side of the Mountain," "It is Well with My Soul," and "Lord Help Me to Hold Out." Ever since times of slavery, our faith has led us to hope. And God gave us this hope because we dared to believe and trust God that as Sam Cooke sang, "A Change Is Gonna Come." Further, the hope found in these songs was put into action, bringing to fruition what we read in James 2 about adding works to our faith.

HARDSHIPS OF SLAVERY

Harriet Jacobs, born and raised in slavery, was taught to read and write and would eventually write about her life as a slave. Jacobs experienced a succession of losses, which included her mother, her mistress, her friend, and her father. When her grandmother told her about the sudden death of her father, her grandmother tried to comfort her with these words: "Who knows the ways of God? Perhaps they have been kindly taken from the evil days to come."[2]

These words have stuck with me because I've often thought this about some of the losses I've experienced. My oldest sister, Angie, died at thirty-two years old, which seemed so cruel. Yet, she'd endured domestic abuse and survived being stabbed more than nine times by her then-husband. I can't help but think her death from cancer, though horrible, was somehow a mercy for the evil that could have come upon her. It's weird to think this way, I know. But it's true—who knows the ways of God? Only God knows.

To say the life of a slave was hard is such an understatement. They often *wished* for death because of what they experienced. And though we live in a time when we are not physically held captive as slaves, we do still experience captivity by our own thoughts and by things that are spoken to us, because we are Black and because we are women. Maybe our hearts are also held captive, unable to fully love or trust one another. For the longest time it was so hard for me to trust others in general, particularly white people, wondering if I'd be blamed if something bad ever happened.

HOPE THROUGH ACTIVISM

Another way to keep hope alive is through activism. What does activism mean, and what does it look like for Christ-followers? It can look like being a conduit for change, a change-maker, and an influencer for the kingdom of God. One thing is for sure: God is always working, and he is always moving. It is up to us to stay close to God and attuned to his spirit to discern how he is moving and to join in his kingdom work.

2 Samuel 21:8-14 tells the story of Rizpah, one of Saul's concubines, who had two sons named Armoni and Mephibosheth. When there was a famine, King David asked the Lord what could be done to receive a reprieve. It turned out that the famine resulted from Saul killing the Gibeonites. In order for the Lord to grant a reprieve, seven sons of Saul—including Rizpah's sons—were to die. They were all killed. For about five months, Rizpah guarded their bodies so they would not be touched by birds or wild animals. Moved by her devotion, King David moved their bones to a proper burial place. Rizpah's story symbolizes mourning and justice, as she demonstrated devotion and courage in the midst of her sorrow by guarding her sons' bodies.

We often hear that we can be activists by voting and participating in the making of laws, and while that's part of it, I believe activism truly starts in our homes and our circles of influence. We are more powerful than we know. Just one Black woman can make a difference—we have seen it time after time. How is the

Lord speaking to you in this area? How can you advocate for yourself and other Black women?

With all that has happened and is happening in our world, it should be no surprise people are looking for hope. The American Psychological Association defines *hope* as "the expectation that one will have positive experiences or that a potentially threatening or negative situation will not materialize or will ultimately result in a favorable state of affairs."[3] Most often when we are hurting, grieving, or suffering, we are hoping and praying that the Lord will just take it away. The author of Proverbs, most likely King Solomon, wrote, "Hope deferred makes the heart sick, but a longing fulfilled is a tree of life" (Proverbs 13:12). I agree: if we don't have hope, we have nothing. Yet, because we have Jesus, we have hope. He is an anchor for our souls. And when all is dark, we can look to the Light of the World to anchor us back to hope again.

SNYDER'S HOPE THEORY

When thinking of ways to put our hands and feet into action, we can consider professor C. R. Snyder's hope theory. This theory defines hope as a way of motivating goal-directed energy and creating ways to meet those goals. This equates to goal-directed determination, deriving a trilogy with *goals*, *pathways*, and *agency* of goal-related thinking.[4] For example, you might set a goal to make a difference in the life of a young Black girl or Black woman. The goal could be to create a scholarship and award it to a recipient, or perhaps to mentor a young Black girl. This approach allows you to change the world one life at a time, contributing to the overall goal of making a difference in the world. This brings you hope because you can see tangible progress. Maybe you have even seen or experienced this firsthand as a mentee or the recipient of a scholarship.

Implementing this goal-oriented theory can stir our hope because it opens the door to so much opportunity. When we think about creating and working toward goals, SMART goals may come to mind. SMART is an acronym to help create reachable, attainable goals—**S**pecific, **M**easurable, **A**chievable, **R**elevant, and **T**ime-bound goals.

It's interesting to consider the concept of SMART goals in relation to the loss and grief we experience as Black women. In particular, it looks like making goals that will have an impact in our communities, our workplaces, our homes, our churches, and anywhere else we operate. What do you think could happen if we applied this concept to the way we navigate loss and grief? I believe it can ignite change agents in us.

HOPE VERSUS FALSE HOPE

Since we are talking about hope, let's tackle the concept of false hope. When I think of false hope, I think of politicians, the shady mechanic who does shoddy work, the not-so-honest car salesman, or the preacher who started the church for money or to meet women. These kinds of people are often shouting things they can't deliver on or don't even believe. It is downright misleading and gives those who will listen false hope.

This is a challenge we face as Black Christian women. At the end of our seeking and searching, if we don't get what we expect, we inevitably become disappointed. And if our unmet expectations and our crushed hopes begin to pile up and we don't see our situation ever turning around, we may descend into hopelessness and despair. If this hopelessness is bottled up, it can turn into anxiety and/or depression with the mindset that things will never change, so why bother. We don't want to go down a dark hole that prevents us from seeing the light. Instead, we can guard against this darkness by knowing the truth of God's Word and by not being swayed by every wind of doctrine (Ephesians 4:14 KJV). We must have discernment and be guided by the Holy Spirit into all truth (John 16:13). And because Hope's name is Jesus, we must draw near to him so that he will draw near to us.

Sometimes it takes help from others to find hope again. Think about all the praying mothers and grandmothers out there. Most of us are where we are today because of someone else helping us along. We are sisters, not enemies. You know it is just like the devil to pit a Black woman against another Black woman, especially Black women of God. I believe the enemy just gets so nervous when he sees us hanging out, working together, strategizing, building things, and empowering one another. But I also believe a lot of the strife that happens between Black women stems from our own insecurities, internalizations, trauma, and negative things that have been spoken over us. When another Black woman walks into the room, we instantly think she's thinking negative thoughts about us—even though we've never met. In those moments, we need to take a breath, step back, and not be ignorant of the devil's devices to divide us and keep us from divine sisterhood. Instead, we can find hope within this community of sisterhood through our shared and individual experiences.

THE STORY OF THE ISRAELITES

There is hope even when we can't see or feel it; it's much like faith. So is there a difference between them? Biblically speaking, hope is a description used for Jesus, the anchor for our soul (Hebrews 6:19). And faith is "the assurance of things hoped for, the conviction of things not seen" (Hebrews 11:1 ESV). Since hope is used in the definition of faith, they go hand in hand.

We find the Exodus story is one of hope. Though it's not void of hardship and the Israelites didn't always get it right, God was faithful to them even when they weren't faithful to him. So much of the story involving the children of Israel, God's chosen people, reminds me of us. For one, we are also God's chosen; he calls us his beloved. We are in his care because we are daughters of the most high God. From captivity, through our desert moments until we reach glory (heaven), our God is for us and with us.

The word *exodus* means liberation, a coming out of the people. Yet, the book of Exodus opens with the new king of Egypt realizing that the Israelites are large in number and are increasing. Fearing what the people will do if war breaks out, he issues a decree to kill all the male Hebrew babies. When that doesn't work, he oppresses them—and even in oppression they still increase in number. Then enters Moses, the one who will deliver them.

The Exodus story reminds me of the fear white people had after emancipation that Black people would seek revenge for their treatment and enslavement. As a result, white people sought other ways to oppress and instill fear into Black people. Yet at the same time, the story of the Israelites is fitting for us as Black people and as Black women because of its inherent hope. Through their struggle, pain, turmoil, doubt, defiance, and suffering, God saw them, was with them, assisted them, and led them to the Promised Land. With glimpses of deliverance and shimmers of his goodness and glory along the way, God gave them something to spur on their hope and faith. In what ways have you seen God show up in your life that made you a little more hopeful?

The Israelite people were in captivity in Egypt for 430 years (Exodus 12:40-41). The length of time they had to endure suffering gives us a different perspective about the things we go through. This is our reminder to allow the Lord more time to work on our behalf.

We can also look at Exodus as a story of resilience in the journey from slavery to the Promised Land. In doing so, we can relate to the in-between places. For the children of Israel, that was the desert. They were crying out to the Lord, "you brought us to the desert to die" (Exodus 14:11). We can see what this desert experience symbolizes in the life of a Black woman: aloneness, dry seasons, being sick and tired of being sick and tired. Have you been there?

THE IN-BETWEEN PLACES

Sometimes the in-between places feel the most unsettling. They are the places of transition, the shift from what once was to what will be. In these places, we wonder, *What am I supposed to do now?* We may feel like we're stuck between a rock and a hard place, unable to go back nor able to move forward.

But let me encourage you today that the in-between place just may be holy ground because God is there. Think about when Moses encountered God at the burning bush: "When the LORD saw that he had gone over to look, God called to him from within the bush, 'Moses! Moses!' And Moses said, 'Here I am.' 'Do not come any closer,' God said. 'Take off your sandals, for the place where you are standing is holy ground'" (Exodus 3:4-5).

Moses was in the in-between place, both literally and spiritually. After leaving Egypt for fear of his life, he traveled far away and ended up in Midian. For Moses, Midian was the place between the enslavement of the Israelites and what God would call him to do to set his people free. The encouragement is this: in the in-between place, God spoke to Moses, and Moses received his calling and purpose.

Jesus also found himself in the in-between place. The time in between Palm Sunday and Easter Sunday—what we call Holy Week. The time between Good Friday and Resurrection Sunday. These were all challenging times that were undeniably excruciating for our Savior. But the in-between place proved to be holy ground, a place of preparation.

When you find yourself in the in-between place, remember you are never alone. Here's what we can take from the Exodus story on what to do:

- ***Cry out to God.*** "During that long period, the king of Egypt died. The Israelites groaned in their slavery and cried out, and their cry for help because of their slavery went up to God. God heard their groaning and he remembered his covenant with Abraham, with Isaac and with Jacob" (Exodus 2:23-24).

- *Make space to hear him.* "The LORD said, 'I have indeed seen the misery of my people in Egypt. I have heard them crying out because of their slave drivers, and I am concerned about their suffering. So I have come down to rescue them from the hand of the Egyptians and to bring them up out of that land into a good and spacious land, a land flowing with milk and honey—the home of the Canaanites, Hittites, Amorites, Perizzites, Hivites and Jebusites'" (Exodus 3:7-8).

- *Allow the Lord to provide.* "Then the LORD said to Moses, 'I will rain down bread from heaven for you. The people are to go out each day and gather enough for that day. In this way, I will test them and see whether they will follow my instructions'" (Exodus 16:4).

- *Rest in God's promise.* "They gave Moses this account: 'We went into the land to which you sent us, and it does flow with milk and honey! Here is its fruit'" (Numbers 13:27).

When we get into a place of despair, we must shift our focus from what's happening around us to what God has done and will do. In this life we will have trouble. That's why it matters where we place our hope. "But those who hope in the LORD will renew their strength. They will soar on wings like eagles;

they will run and not grow weary, they will walk and not be faint" (Isaiah 40:31).

THE WIDOW OF ZAREPHATH

As we come to the end of this conversation on how hope matters, let's explore the story of a widow. The prophet Jeremiah introduces us to the widow of Zarephath, whom God showed great care for. She lived in a time of famine and was down to her last resources. Jeremiah wrote, "Some time later the brook dried up because there had been no rain in the land" (1 Kings 17:7). There is just something about God meeting us in dry places. Do you see a theme here?

The widow was out gathering sticks so she could go home to keep her son warm. She expected them both to die. She had no clue she was being set up for a miracle. But Elijah the prophet met her, gave her a promise from God, and God ended up providing oil and flour for the widow, her son, and Elijah for as long as the famine lasted.

Sometimes this is where we find ourselves, too, with no clue we're being set up for a miracle. We are ready to give up, we are at our wit's end, and we have done all we can do. Amid this grief, we don't know where to go from here nor how we will make it through the next week, the next day, or the next hour. And sometimes I wonder if that's where God wants us, where we come to the end of ourselves such that we reach for him. It's not that he wants us to go through hard things, but more so that he uses the hard things to work his plans and purpose in us. Jeremiah wrote, "'For I know the plans I have for you,' declares the LORD, 'plans to prosper you and not to harm you, plans to give you hope and a future'" (Jeremiah 29:11). We know that behind the scenes our God is working on our behalf. He has miracles on the other side.

What especially struck me about this story is how the widow of Zarephath did what she could for her son until the end, which is what Black women do. In trusting God, both she and her son lived (1 Kings 17:15-16). By trusting God and placing our hope in him, we too can live with hope in this grief-filled world.

Dear Black woman,

I won't even lie—sometimes hope seems fleeting, like when we were little and we used to try to catch fireflies in a jar. We played out in the yard with our friends until it started to get dark and the fireflies would come out. Then we'd run around with whatever we could find to catch them. We'd see the fireflies light up and excitedly approach them with our jar, only to find out with a sinking heart that we missed them. Sometimes hope feels like that.

But what I've come to know is that hope is real. And if and when we grab on to hope, it really can change the trajectory of our lives. Hope matters. So hold on to hope and don't let it go.

11

FAITH MARCHES ON

*Faith is what makes life bearable, with all its tragedies
and ambiguities and sudden, startling joys.*

MADELEINE L'ENGLE

HAVE YOU EVER CRIED SO MUCH that your eyes were nearly
swollen shut as if you had a bad allergy flare-up? I cried so hard
after my first big breakup, when I placed my baby in adoptive
care senior year of high school, after the death of my sister
Angie, when I got the call of my sister Sharon's cancer diag-
nosis and then her death, when my dad died, when my nephew
Anthony was murdered, when my unborn children died due to
miscarriage and stillbirth, and when my church split.

Maybe you didn't shed tears in your situation, but you still
experienced a deep aching of the soul, a hollowing out of your
heart, because of a church divided over politics and racial
injustices, a divorce, a promotion for which you were overlooked, unmet dreams or expectations, prayers that seemed to
reach only as far as the ceiling. Maybe it's because of a snarky

comment that made you question your beauty or your intellect. Or a gesture, look, or tone that made you feel othered, dejected, or rejected. Or sleepless nights over a loved one or friend who is struggling mentally, physically, or spiritually.

With all that has taken place in your life, do you ever just sit and ponder, *Where would I be if Jesus was not with me?* Seriously, take a moment to sit with this question.

I'm thirty-plus years into this grief journey. And I'm still journeying. Through it all, my faith has been my anchor. I can't say that I have always seen it while I was in it. But that's faith, right? Think about the scene after Jesus' resurrection when he appears to his disciples. When they tell Thomas, he's like: Wait a minute, how do I *really* know it was the Lord you saw? He declares that unless he can see the nail marks in Jesus' hands and put his fingers where the nails were, he won't believe it's really him (John 20:25). When Jesus appears to the disciples again with Thomas present, Jesus tells him to do just that so he will believe. But take note of what the Lord tells Thomas: "Because you have seen me, you have believed; blessed are those who have not seen and yet have believed" (John 20:29).

The thing about faith is that we have to believe it before we see it. We have to believe the Lord is making a way for us in the desert, that he is water for us in a dry and weary land, and that he has already made provision for us in a world that seems to be against us.

Having faith is important in the grief journey. We need faith to believe God is close to the brokenhearted. We need faith to believe God will never leave us nor forsake us. We need faith when the grief is pounding unceasingly. When it feels as though our situation is larger than our faith, we can be reminded that faith the size of a mustard seed moves mountains (Matthew 17:20). The faith that saved us when we accepted Jesus into our hearts is the same faith that carries us through the loss and grief we experience in this life. It is by faith in the Lord's great compassion that we are not consumed by our loss and grief (Lamentations 3:22).

Holding on to our faith amid grief is like setting our faces like flint (Isaiah 50:7), being unmoving, unwavering, and always abiding in Christ. However, this doesn't always look the way you might expect. Grief is the unexpected enemy that somehow becomes an unexpected companion.

WRESTLING THROUGH GRIEF

In her book *Conscious Grieving*, therapist and author Claire Bidwell Smith discusses three intervals of grief that may help inform you on your journey:

1. *Acute grief*—This stage incorporates earlier grief and describes the numbness we may feel at the onset of the loss. An example may be our initial reaction to an injustice, such as how we felt when we heard of the George Floyd case.

2. *Active grief*—This stage incorporates reminders or anniversaries and how we respond to them. This may include reminders from another racially motivated incident or death on the news or the anniversary of the death of a loved one.

3. *After grief*—This stage refers to the grief we may feel throughout our lifetime. As Black women, we live in a constant state of grief. This stage also points to how we function in the world after the loss has occurred and the meaning we make from the grief we have experienced.[1]

In thinking about continuing this grief journey, I love the idea of marking our losses as a practical way of acknowledging and processing them. In a conversation I had with Sarah Bell, a grief educator and hospice chaplain, she talked about how she hadn't allowed herself to fully grieve the loss of her baby. One day she decided to mark the loss by having a little ceremony for the baby in which she buried a pair of baby shoes. Instead of saying, "Oh, that didn't hurt," perhaps we also need to mark our losses to fully grieve them.

Amid grief, our minds may wrestle with the question "How long, LORD?" just as David did in Psalm 13:1. How long before I get a reprieve from this pain, grief, and suffering? How long before I feel seen, heard, and understood? How long will it take for me to love and see myself as you love and see me, Lord? It is healthy to be curious, to ask questions, and to wrestle with God. In Genesis 32, Jacob wrestled with God as well.

I love this from Cole Arthur Riley in her book *Black Liturgies*: "May our mourning look how it must from one moment to the next, free from guilt about how much sadness we can muster."[2] God is not looking down on us as we experience loss and grief, saying, "I don't know what I'm going to do with her." No, he is making intercession for us and lovingly singing over us as we wrestle through.

GRACE FOR THE JOURNEY

When I think of the presence of grief in my life, Paul's account of the thorn in his flesh comes to mind: "Therefore, in order to keep me from becoming conceited, I was given a thorn in my flesh, a messenger of Satan, to torment me. Three times I pleaded with the Lord to take it away from me. But he said to me, 'My grace is sufficient for you, for my power is made perfect in weakness'" (2 Corinthians 12:7-9).

This thorn in the flesh symbolizes how we learn to navigate through, in, and around our grief. As Paul reminds us, God's grace is sufficient for us in our grief. And though our pains and struggles linger, our faith marches on.

I never knew how much I needed God until I experienced deep loss and grief. Each loss, instead of pushing me away from God, drew me closer to him because I was trusting him for what he says, not what I see. Jesus' entire healing ministry was built on the foundation of faith. Our very Christian belief is built on trusting in a God we do not see. We are trusting him to hold us in the palm of his hand when the loss and grief of being a Black woman in America tugs at the threads of our sanity.

In *Emotionally Healthy Spirituality*, Peter Scazzero says that every Christian at some point will confront the wall, or "the night of the soul."[3] As you continue on this grief journey as a Black woman, there will come a point when you confront a loss or a hard place that seems insurmountable—and moving forward, you will likely continue to meet walls of resistance. My prayer is that you will be able to use this book as a resource for a breakthrough or a way through. We are better suited to confront these walls when our hearts are malleable to God's Spirit, his presence, and his Word. Instead of repeatedly coming up against the wall of defeat, we will be able to lift a shout of victory to our God.

I once heard someone say, "Don't let what happens to you get inside of you." Essentially, don't let the bad things that happen to you harden your heart. God already knows the things we will encounter in this life that will harden our hearts, and he has made provision for us because he always makes a way of escape for us. How does he do this? By turning our hearts of stone into hearts of flesh (Ezekiel 36:26) so that we will have open hands, an open heart, open ears, and open eyes to receive all he has for us during seasons of loss and grief. God is always with us, he is always speaking, and he is waiting for us to tune into his presence.

FAITH FOR THE JOURNEY

Hebrews 11:1 says, "Now faith is confidence in what we hope for and assurance about what we do not see." Faith embraces the Word of God. Though life is challenging and grief may knock us down, we believe that all of God's promises are yes and amen. To be open to a move of God on our behalf, to see his power in our life, our eyes and ears must be open to him. Keep in mind that breakthrough, as it relates to grief, can look different depending on the circumstances. Maybe it's a reprieve from the tangible pain you've been feeling since the loss. Or maybe you received the promotion you never thought you'd get despite coming against opposition.

Let's take a look at the six stages of faith for Black women.

Stage 1: Being aware of the resurgent and constant state of grief. This stage reflects a profound understanding of the collective and intergenerational trauma experienced within the Black community. It signifies a recognition of the ongoing impact of historical injustices, systemic oppression, and racial violence, which continue to reverberate through individual lives and communities. In this stage, we may grapple with the weight of inherited grief, acknowledging the pain passed down through generations while also confronting our own experiences of loss and struggle. This awareness fosters a deep sense of empathy, solidarity, and resilience, as we draw strength from our shared history and collective struggle for justice and liberation. Moreover, this stage of faith underscores the importance of healing and restoration as we navigate the complexities of grief, trauma, and resilience. It prompts a spiritual journey toward healing, reconciliation, and empowerment, as we seek to honor our ancestors, reclaim our identities, and cultivate hope for a more just and equitable future.

Stage 2: Developing our character through hardship. This stage embodies a profound journey of spiritual growth and resilience. In the face of systemic inequalities, racial injustices, and personal adversities, we navigate the complexities of our experiences with unwavering strength and determination. This stage involves confronting and transcending obstacles, whether they stem from societal oppression or individual challenges, to cultivate a steadfast character grounded in integrity, perseverance, and empathy. Through adversity, we deepen our understanding of ourselves, our communities, and our spirituality, drawing on our faith to find meaning, purpose, and hope amid hardship. This journey of character development not only shapes our individual identities but also contributes to the collective resilience of the Black community, inspiring others to persevere and thrive in the face of adversity.

Stage 3. Serving through pain. This stage represents a profound commitment to faith, community, and resilience in the face of adversity. Despite experiencing personal and systemic challenges, we embrace a higher calling to serve others, channeling pain into purposeful action and compassion. This stage involves navigating the complexities of suffering, whether from racial injustices, personal hardships, or societal trauma, and using these experiences to empathize with and support those in need. Through our acts of service, we embody a profound sense of solidarity, healing, and empowerment, uplifting our communities and advocating for justice and equity. Serving through pain is not only a testament to our unwavering faith and strength but also a transformative journey of spiritual growth, empowerment, and collective liberation.

Stage 4: Experiencing a crisis of faith. When questions arise—like *Where is God? Has God turned a blind eye to all the injustice? Has God abandoned us? Do we matter?*—we must try to understand what is happening inside of us because of our constant grief and mourning for ourselves and our communities. This stage represents a pivotal moment of introspection, questioning, and spiritual growth. In the face of systemic injustices, personal struggles, and societal pressures, Black women may find themselves grappling with doubts, uncertainties, and existential dilemmas about their beliefs and spirituality. This stage involves confronting the complexities of faith and identity, navigating the tensions between religious teachings and lived experiences, and wrestling with profound existential questions about the nature of suffering, justice, and divine purpose.

During a crisis of faith, we may experience feelings of doubt, disillusionment, and alienation from our religious communities or spiritual practices. We may question longstanding beliefs, challenge traditional interpretations of Scripture, and seek new avenues for spiritual understanding and meaning. This period of upheaval and uncertainty can be deeply unsettling and challenging, yet it also offers an opportunity for profound self-discovery, growth, and transformation. Ultimately, this stage of faith invites us to embrace the complexities of our spiritual journey, trusting in our ability to navigate uncertainty and emerge with a stronger, more resilient faith.

Stage 5: Resisting the culture. In this stage we embrace Christ, his plan, and his eternal purposes. We can resist cultural norms and embrace the kingdom of God, which signifies a transformative journey of spiritual empowerment and liberation. Amid societal pressures and systemic injustices that marginalize and devalue Black women, we assert our agency and identity by aligning with the values of God's kingdom. Rejecting narratives of inferiority, we reclaim our dignity and worth as beloved children of God, advocating for social change and working toward a world where all are valued and affirmed. Grounded in the teachings of Jesus, we find strength and hope in our spiritual identity, embodying principles of love, compassion, and justice as we actively engage in the ongoing work of building a more equitable society.

Stage 6: Spurring on the next generation. This stage is a profound commitment to mentorship, empowerment, and legacy building. Rooted in the rich cultural traditions and resilience of the Black community, we as Black women actively invest in nurturing and uplifting future generations by passing down wisdom, values, and aspirations. This stage involves serving as role models, advocates, and mentors to empower young Black women to embrace their identity, pursue their dreams, and overcome obstacles. Through our guidance and support, we can inspire resilience, courage, and leadership in the next generation, fostering a legacy of strength, excellence, and empowerment that transcends generations and uplifts the entire community.

The journey of faith for Black women is dynamic and multifaceted, marked by resilience, empowerment, and spiritual growth. From the foundational stage of cultural immersion to the transformative stages of resistance and liberation, we navigate the complexities of our faith with unwavering strength, determination, and grace. Thus, our faith journey is not only a personal odyssey of self-discovery but also a collective narrative that continues to shape the fabric of our communities and inspire generations to come.

Dear Black woman,

The truth is this journey of grief will continue. Yet
with every twist and turn in the road, it is also true
that you are not alone. You are more equipped than
you once were. You are walking in the confidence of
God, who holds you in any loss you encounter. You
are leaning into the truth of God's Word, and with
faith even the size of a mustard seed, you will see
mountains move. You are confident that your faith
heals and makes you whole. God is affirming his
truth in your life as you read his Word, listen for his
voice, and walk by faith in the steps he has ordered
for you. He will indeed complete the work he has
begun in your life.

12

HEALING AND WHOLENESS

The Black female is assaulted in her tender years
by all those common forces of nature at the same time that
she is caught in the tripartite crossfire of masculine prejudice,
white illogical hate, and Black lack of power.
The fact that the adult American Negro female emerges
as a formidable character is often met with
amazement, distaste, and even belligerence.

It is seldom accepted as an inevitable outcome
of the struggle won by survivors and deserves
respect if not enthusiastic acceptance.

DR. MAYA ANGELOU

IN THE SUMMER OF 2023, the blockbuster film *Barbie*
grabbed the attention of millions of people. One of the
most talked about moments of the film was a monologue by
America Ferrera's character, Gloria, which starts with the
heart-wrenching statement, "It is literally impossible to be a
woman." This monologue had me sitting still in my seat as

tears welled in my eyes and fell to my cheeks. All I could think about was how true it was, especially being a Black woman on top of everything.

The intersection of race and gender is often a double whammy for us. Mary Church Terrell, the first Black woman to serve on a board of education, said, "A white woman has only one handicap to overcome—a great one, true, her sex: a colored woman faces two—her sex and her race. A colored man has only one—that of race. Colored women are the only group in this country who have two heavy handicaps to overcome."[1]

Too often, others have benefited from our insecurity, our brokenness, and our perception of our self-worth. But we deserve to be healed and whole. I recently recommended counseling to a friend, as I had been seeing one myself. She admitted to being somewhat resistant because of the stigma surrounding the idea of seeking help. Counseling isn't for the weak; it is a helping hand. It allows us to process what we are going through and provides a safe place to express and release what we have been carrying on the inside. The more we know, the more we grow.

There's a meme floating around that says something like, "You are always taking care of everyone else, but who is going to take care of you?" There is another one that says, "No one is coming for you"—meaning no one is coming to help you. Oof. The sentiment is drab, but there is some truth to it in terms of how we sometimes feel alone and isolated.

Having this mindset that we have to do everything ourselves can lead us to run around like a headless chicken trying to do all the things. I'll pause here to share that I have seen a chicken with its head cut off. Growing up, one of our neighbors started raising chickens from the cutest little yellow chicks. When the chickens were grown, my family went to our neighbor's house to help kill the chickens. I remember they were submerged into boiling water to aid in the removal of the feathers, which we kids helped with. Anyway, the moral of this story is that we should not get to a point where we are running aimlessly all over the place, only to be put in boiling water and pulled apart. If that wasn't the weirdest analogy, I don't know what is. But in a way, this is the reality for Black women.

COMMON COPING STRATEGIES

How Black women have coped with hardship in the past can provide insight into the ways we may be currently coping. There are several roles that Black women have historically taken on.

- *Sojourner syndrome.* Black women who are resilient are more likely to hold in their stress, fight, or "explode" than discuss their problems with others. Other coping strategies associated with this role are overeating or over-working to alleviate stress.

- *Strong Black woman.* This kind of Black woman internalizes social expectations by caring for others over herself. (See chapter one for a more detailed description.)

- *Superwoman schema.* This refers to Black women who help others before themselves, achieve success no matter the cost, appear strong, suppress their feelings, and avoid being seen as vulnerable or dependent on others.

- *Sisterella complex.* This explains how internalized racism, sexism, and harmful coping strategies can lead Black women to experience depression and other mental challenges.[2]

After reading these, which do you identify most with? I most relate to the superwoman schema, but I can also see myself in the others. Knowing these can help us become more self-aware so we can begin to take needed steps toward healing and wholeness.

Part of self-care is allowing yourself to grieve the losses you've experienced. Pause to make space for grief with this exercise.

1. *Acknowledge.* Name the loss. You can list the death of a loved one, a racial injustice, or whatever loss you are tending to at this moment. For example, I was angry and felt like I had lost time after seven months of carrying a baby with nothing to show for it.

2. *Assign.* Assign a feeling to this loss. We can expand our language when it comes to grief. We are more than just mad, glad, happy, or sad. If you can't find the words, consult the Feelings Wheel for suggestions.

3. *Affirm.* I am (insert feeling), yet God (Scripture affirming God's character). We are not replacing our feelings. Instead, we acknowledge them and invite God into how this loss is affecting us so he can help us where we are. This also reminds us of who God is.

FEELINGS WHEEL

Mad — Hurt, Hostile, Angry, Rage, Hateful, Critical

Scared — Confused, Rejected, Helpless, Submissive, Insecure, Anxious

Joyful — Excited, Sexy, Energetic, Playful, Creative, Aware

Powerful — Proud, Respected, Appreciated, Hopeful, Important, Faithful

Peaceful — Nurturing, Trusting, Loving, Intimate, Thoughtful, Content

Sad — Sleepy, Bored, Lonely, Depressed, Ashamed, Guilty

Jealous, Selfish, Frustrated, Furious, Irritated, Skeptical, Bewildered, Discouraged, Insignificant, Weak, Foolish, Embarrassed, Daring, Fascinating, Stimulating, Amused, Extravagant, Delightful, Cheerful, Satisfied, Valuable, Worthwhile, Intelligent, Confident, Thankful, Sentimental, Serene, Responsive, Relaxed, Pensive, Apathetic, Inferior, Inadequate, Miserable, Stupid, Bashful

SELF-CARE ISN'T SELFISH

I originally didn't want to address self-care in this book. Maybe it's because I'm terrible at it or because part of me thinks it's overrated. But to be honest, I haven't really tried it. And the more I got to thinking about it, the more I started to wonder, *Why* haven't *I tried getting into self-care?* After all, I do feel recharged after taking time for myself.

In thinking about why it's so hard to engage in self-care, the word *self* stands out to me. You've probably seen the phrase "self-care isn't selfish" on social media. Yet, I often find that after doing just one thing for myself, I have the urge to explain away all the reasons why I deserved it.

I once saw an Instagram reel of a Black woman seated on a chair with her arms folded. As soon as she heard her husband's footsteps approaching, she proceeded to act like she was busy doing something else. I'm embarrassed to admit that I've been guilty of doing this with my husband and my kids. (I hope they don't read this part.) This is the mindset that taking a break means we either don't have much going on or we could be making better use of our time doing something else.

I've come to understand this as a type of trauma response. I remember being scolded as a child, "Don't just stand there, do something!" Deep down, we don't believe we deserve a break. We think we are being selfish when we take time to do something just for ourselves. It's as if we need permission to engage in self-care, waiting for someone to say, "You've earned a break."

There is also a lack of modeling of self-care for Black women. While I was growing up, my mom was often exhausted, drained, and super irritable. Yet even in her tiredness, she continued working, helping, and volunteering in the home, with her family, at church, and in the community. Now as a grown Black woman, I can relate. I never saw my mom rest, and even now in her early eighties, she still can't get the full rest she desires because she commits most of her time to caring for her mother. Though I'm not the best at self-care, my prayer is that I can be honest and open about it with my daughters so they will take notice and allow themselves time and opportunity to rest.

SELF-CARE ASSESSMENT

The most prevalent excuses for not engaging in self-care include feeling like we don't have enough time, feeling guilty, and coming up against structural barriers. Maybe we even think self-care is not feasible because we're Black women. Let's explore this for a bit. This urge to keep going until the wheels fall off is driven by the mindset that we have to work three times as hard as everyone else just so others will treat us with respect.

What can we do right now to evaluate our perspective on self-care? Ask yourself these ten questions to self-assess.

1. What am I thankful for?
2. What action do I take to refuel, refresh, unwind?
3. When I hear the phrase *self-care*, what comes to mind?
4. Am I hesitant in thinking about self-care?
5. Where am I hurting?
6. Where am I healing?
7. Where do I find the most support?
8. Where am I holding sorrow?
9. Where am I holding joy?
10. Have I allowed myself to grieve the losses I've experienced?

What are your answers telling you about your self-care? What area(s) can you improve on, make changes in, or do more of?

We often have a limited understanding of self-care; we think it's just going to a spa and getting a manicure, pedicure, or facial. However, there is self-care we can do that doesn't cost any money. Most importantly, it is invaluable because it helps us mentally. Research suggests self-care began in the field of nursing and defines it as the self-application of activities to regulate health apart from systemic health care. "Some health-related literature has recommended practices like deep breathing and meditation for Black women's self-care-related needs like stress management, health improvement, self-awareness, and finding purpose."[3]

One way to engage in self-care is by setting boundaries. Here are a few ways to do so.

- *Identify your limits.* Reflect on your needs, values, and limits to determine what boundaries are important to you in various areas of your life, such as relationships, work, and personal time.

- *Learn to say no.* It's okay to say no to requests or commitments that don't align with your boundaries or priorities. Practice saying no politely but firmly, without feeling guilty or obligated to justify your decision.

- *Set consequences.* Establish consequences for boundary violations and follow through with them if necessary. Consistent consequences reinforce the importance of your boundaries and encourage respect from others.

- *Regularly reevaluate.* Periodically reassess your boundaries and make adjustments as needed based on changes in circumstances or priorities. Flexibility allows you to adapt your boundaries to meet your evolving needs.

- *Seek support.* Surround yourself with supportive individuals who respect your boundaries and encourage you to prioritize self-care. Having a supportive network can help reinforce your boundaries and provide validation when needed.

EMBRACING SOUL CARE

I believe soul care and self-care go hand in hand. Barbara Peacock, author of *Soul Care in African American Practice*, discusses three disciplines that help with spiritual growth: prayer, spiritual direction, and soul care. She writes,

> The language of soul is not new but has been around for thousands of years. The African American community has used soul in song, communal language, poetry, and so on. Therefore, readings and teachings developed around the concept of "soul care," as opposed to "spiritual direction," may be more readily accepted in our faith communities. . . . For sure, the greatest spiritual director is our Lord and Savior Jesus Christ, and without a doubt, no person can provide better direction than he.[4]

Connecting with the Lord is the key to caring for our soul.

Two spiritual practices I'd like to mention were introduced to me by my sweet friend and fellow author, Terra McDaniel, in her book *Hopeful Lament*. The first is the tearing practice, in which you use the act of tearing material, whether paper or cloth, to physically express grief and emotion. In the tear jar practice, dropping grains of salt into a jar of water allows you to outwardly express tears even if you are too numb to do so yourself. I have found both to be powerful, beautiful, and simple yet effective practices.[5]

Thinking further about ways we tend to our self and soul brings the Black community to mind. As a student on a predominantly white college campus, I was part of a Black community that had been intentionally created, curated, and cultivated to help students on campus feel less isolated and alone. Even before the overall student orientation, the university provided an African American Symposium for students of color. To say the least, this community was very impactful for students who studied and lived out their college years together. It was so beautiful, and I wish there was more of this now for adults post-college. It is up to us to either find these communities or create our own.

My healing journey has involved cultivating and engaging in a safe community. I admit that I initially didn't want to be part of one because of how I'd been hurt in the past. But once I found people who truly cared about me and started the journey of healing and wholeness that God wanted for me, there was nothing better.

So how do we find community and sisterhood? We can look to the age-old rule of Proverbs 18:24: you have to show yourself friendly if you want friends. Again, having been hurt in the past made it a challenge for me to fully trust people for some time. Yet, as we continue on this healing journey, we are able to open up and be a bit more vulnerable to engage in conversations with other Black women such that more healing can happen. James wrote, "Therefore confess your sins to each other and pray for each other so that you may be healed. The prayer of a righteous person is powerful and effective" (James 5:16).

Lastly, we can engage in healing through advocacy work. The Black Girl Magic and Black Girl Joy movements, which appeared on Twitter (now X) in 2011, were both created to celebrate the awesome things Black girls and women have done and continue to do through expressions of positivity, empowerment, encouragement, and permission to live lives full of joy.[6] I don't know about you, but I love to see another Black woman win. Who else will cheer us on if we don't do so for each other?

THE ARMOR OF GOD

The Bible gives us the ability to combat hard things and armor up spiritually. However, sometimes we get into the mindset that what we do doesn't matter or doesn't count. If we pray, will it change things? If we ask for protection over our family, will it happen? It goes back to our willingness to believe that God is not like man. We have a hard time trusting men because *they* have let us down time and time again. This skepticism often stems from our experiences with unreliable human relationships, especially if we have a strained relationship with our earthly father, which can leave deep emotional wounds. These wounds influence how we relate to God, others, and our beliefs about spiritual practices like prayer. I hope that the following tools and practices will help you live fully engaged with God and Scripture in order to experience his fullness and the life he intended for you even while living in this grief-filled world.

The Bible isn't short on providing us with what we need for every area of life, including healing. When we think of healing, we often think of the absence of pain with everything nice and neat as it once was, or we think that healing is spontaneous. However, this usually isn't the case. Healing often takes time and requires us to do our part. God will always bring healing, though it may not look like what we expect.

Second Kings 5:1-15 tells the story of Naaman, a commander of the king's army, who was healed of leprosy. The prophet Elisha sent a messenger to tell Naaman he would be restored if he washed himself seven times in the Jordan (2 Kings 5:10). Expecting to be healed in a different manner, Naaman quickly became angry (2 Kings 5:11). When Naaman's servant saw his anger, he helped him consider if the method in which he received his healing was as important as being healed. Thus, Naaman changed his mind and decided to follow the Lord's instruction to go wash and be cleansed. When we are waiting on God for healing, we too can easily become angry and frustrated. Naaman's story is an encouragement to stay the course, reminding us that healing will come in ways we can't even imagine.

Sometimes, putting what we know into practice can feel daunting, awkward, or even, if we are honest, like nonvaluable activities. But when we activate the Word of God, we discover that something truly does happen, even if we don't immediately sense or see it. I'm reminded of Martin Luther King Jr.'s approach to the chaotic world we live in: "It is not enough to say 'We must not wage war.' It is necessary to love peace and sacrifice for it. We must concentrate not merely on the negative expulsion of war, but the positive affirmation of peace."[7]

Paul wrote, "Finally, be strong in the Lord and in his mighty power. Put on the full armor of God, so that you can take your stand against the devil's schemes" (Ephesians 6:10-11). The armor of God equips us to be on the offense while still recognizing that the Lord fights our battles. It's necessary to understand that the battles we fight in this world are also spiritual. Further, we can look at the armor of God as a road map for navigating grief as Black women in America and as a pathway to hope, healing, and wholeness. A road map helps us navigate, provides us tips for the journey, helps us plan ahead, and gives us the bigger picture.

Using the armor of God, let's explore three roads that will help lead us to healing and wholeness.

Be strong in the Lord and in his power. In chapter one, we discussed how we were never meant to be strong by our own might. The story of David and Goliath demonstrates this. When they fought, David said to Goliath, "You come against me with sword and spear and javelin, but I come against you in the name of the LORD Almighty, the God of the armies of Israel, whom you have defied. This day the LORD will deliver you into my hands, and I'll strike you down and cut off your head" (1 Samuel 17:45-46). David encouraged himself in the Lord, remembering that his victories were because of God's help and strength.

Put on the whole armor of God and stand. These pieces are described in Ephesians 6 as follows:

- Belt of truth—to keep the Word of God centered in our lives
- Breastplate of righteousness—to guard our hearts
- Shoes with the preparation of the gospel of peace—to let the Holy Spirit be our guide
- Shield of faith—to protect us against the attacks of our heart
- Helmet of salvation—to guard our mind and our thoughts
- Sword of the Spirit—the Word of God

Pray always. Prayer is one of the most underestimated gifts and powerful spiritual practices in the life of the Christ follower. I love this quote from writer Madeleine L'Engle:

> I will have nothing to do with a God who cares only occasionally. I need a God who is with us always, everywhere, in the deepest depths as well as the highest heights. It is when things go wrong, when good things do not happen, when our prayers seem to have been lost, that God is most present. We do not need the sheltering wings when things go smoothly. We are closest to God in the darkness, stumbling along blindly.[8]

God is with us, and he listens to and answers our prayers. At the church where I grew up, we used to have prayer meetings. Someone would start singing a song the Lord had laid on their heart, and one by one, everyone else would join in. I have to be honest—as a seven-year-old, the thought of going to prayer meetings was boring. But when I was there it felt like peace, as the sanctuary was mainly filled with Black women giving prayer requests, praying, and sharing testimonies.

The power of prayer only became more evident to me as I grew older. The United Student Fellowship I was part of in college held weekly prayer meetings on campus. We took an hour to meet in a classroom and pray. When people entered the room, they would go directly to the chalkboard and write down their prayer requests so everyone in the room could pray in agreement over those requests. This is a beautiful example of how a community can come together in prayer to change things. And let me tell you, there were so many prayers answered, including the salvation of many of my loved ones.

Prayer is communication with God. In prayer, we bring our praise, our thanksgiving, and our requests to the Lord. We spend time with God, casting the whole of our cares on him because he cares for us like no one else can. "Now this is the confidence that we have in Him, that if we ask anything according to His will, He hears us. And if we know that He hears us, whatever we ask, we know that we have the petitions that we have asked of Him" (1 John 5:14-15 NKJV).

Big things happen in the Bible as a result of prayer, but don't discount the small things, either. The prophet Elijah prayed for rain and it happened (1 Kings 18:41). God had already promised rain, which means Elijah was praying the promise of God. When we study our Bible, we see that God has promised us so much. We too can pray according to the promises of God, "For no matter how many promises God has made, they are

'Yes' in Christ. And so through him the 'Amen' is spoken by us to the glory of God" (2 Corinthians 1:20).

Remember God's promises. Remembering God's promises helps us in hard times, in loss, and in grief. We can pray these promises of God over ourselves, our children, our friends, and our families.

- We are never alone or abandoned. (Deuteronomy 31:6)
- He is close to us. (Psalm 34:18)
- He provides for us. (Psalm 23:1)
- He helps us. (Psalm 46:1)
- He fights for us. (Exodus 14:14)
- He protects us. (Psalm 28:7)
- He satisfies us with a long life. (Psalm 91:16)
- He gives us wisdom. (James 1:5-7)
- We are free in Christ. (John 8:36)
- We are his children. (John 1:12)

Dear Black woman,

You are loved. You are beautiful. You are capable of healing and wholeness. What you have gone through or what you are even now experiencing is not an indication of who you are or who God is. You are covered and surrounded by God's everlasting love. Let his love be a shield around you, guarding you from the ways the grief and trauma of the world can harden your heart against the Lord and others.

Remember your strength lies in knowing who you are in Christ, knowing that in him you can do all things and that all things are possible when you believe. Remember that your faith and hope are rooted and anchored in the Lord. It is this foundation that will keep you steady when the world is shifting and it feels as if you are sinking. God has made your feet like hinds' feet to stand and to climb, and he has made your hands ready for war. You are already equipped for the battle. Yet God in his loving care reminds you that he is with you to fight your battles. You are just to be still, armored up and ready to heed what the Spirit of the Lord is calling you to.

May we have eyes to see and ears to hear what the Spirit is speaking to us as we continue this journey of healing and wholeness. As the prophet Jeremiah wrote, "Heal me, LORD, and I will be healed; save me and I will be saved, for you are the one I praise" (Jeremiah 17:14).

ACKNOWLEDGMENTS

THIS BOOK IS THE BOOK I didn't want to write but knew I needed to write. I'm grateful for the hope and healing it brought me during the research and writing stages. And I'm grateful for the opportunity to have the words within these pages bring hope, help, and healing to other Black women.

To my prayer team, who came together to pray for me from a belief in the work God is doing in and through me—thank you. To Martha, you are my people. I love talking about all things with you. Thank you for your encouragement throughout my writing journey and your prayers. I'm so grateful for your pastoral leadership and your friendship. To my sweet friend Vivian, who prays for me on demand, any time I ask. To Viv and Robin, thank you for your friendship and your prayers during the writing of this book. To my grief group members, thank you for your prayers. I'm so grateful for each of you.

To my editor, Nilwona, thank you for your keen eye, gentle nudges, and encouraging words throughout this process. It helped bring so much richness to these pages. To the entire team at InterVarsity Press, you are simply the best. Thank you for believing in me for another book.

To my literary agent, Mary DeMuth—something just happens when someone has the gift of drawing out what God has placed in someone else. Mary, you have that gift. I'm so very grateful for you saying yes to my query letter, for believing in my words and my work, and for bringing this book out of me.

To my mom, Willie, thank you for your love and sacrifice and for always pointing me to the One who keeps us in all things. I love you so much. To my sister Charlotte, it's just me and you as we often say. I'm so grateful we have been able to spend such sweet moments together. I love you to the moon and back. Let's make a difference in this world together.

To my Aunt Doris, who told me about all the books I would write before I even had any idea about writing them, thank you for listening to the voice of God. I love you so much. To my niece Nicole, you're like my little sister. Thank you for your unfailing support of everything I do. I love you so much.

To my mother- and sister-in-law, Shirley and Charmaine, thank you so much for your support of my work. To my nephews and nieces, Jeffrey, George, Gregory, Jamez, and Yahzmein, thank you for allowing me to speak into your lives. I love you so much. To all my family near and far who support me in any way, I'm so very grateful.

To my best friends Margaret and Tasha, who inspire me, who get me, and who I can send a text to in a hot minute about anything, I'm so grateful to have you in my life. When we talk about friends who have been there from the start, you are it. I love you ladies. To my writer friends new and old who consistently show up for me in ways I couldn't have imagined, I'm so very grateful for you.

To my children, Emma, Tre', Christian, and Isabella. You are such a treasure. I am so grateful for each one of you. Even at your age, you inspire me. Thank you for the hugs, smiles, laughter, and encouragement. You are all world changers.

To my husband, Clinton, you have been such an encouraging force throughout this writing journey. You constantly affirm God's call and purpose in my life even when I question it. Thank you for your leading voice that points me to God's plans. I'm so grateful for you and so honored to be your wife. I love you so much.

To my Lord and Savior Jesus Christ, I am a living testament of how you call the unqualified and qualify the called. I'm forever grateful, Lord, for you choosing me as your daughter and to be used for such a time as this.

NOTES

FOREWORD

[1] See Cheryl Woods-Giscombe, Millicent Nicolle Robinson, Dana Carthon, Stephanie Devane-Johnson, and Giselle Corbie-Smith, "Superwoman Schema, Stigma, Spirituality, and Culturally Sensitive Providers: Factors Influencing African American Women's Use of Mental Health Services," National Library of Medicine, *J Best Pract Health Prof Divers*, 2016 Spring, 9(1): 1124–1144.

INTRODUCTION

[1] Da'Mere T. Wilson and Mary-Frances O'Connor, "From Grief to Grievance: Combined Axes of Personal and Collective Grief Among Black Americans," *Frontiers in Psychiatry*, 13 (2022): 850994, https://doi.org/10.3389/fpsyt.2022.850994.

[2] Natasha Smith, *Can You Just Sit with Me?: Healthy Grieving for the Losses of Life* (Downers Grove, IL: InterVarsity Press, 2023), 19.

[3] Saba Mughal, Yusra Azhar, Margaret M. Mahon, and Waqas J. Siddiqui, *Grief Reaction and Prolonged Grief Disorder* (Treasure Island, FL: StatPearls Publishing, 2024), www.ncbi.nlm.nih.gov/books/NBK507832/.

[4] Mughal et al., *Grief Reaction and Prolonged Grief Disorder.*

1. STRONG BLACK WOMAN

[1] Alesha Lackey, "The Fallacy of the Strong Black Woman," Charlotte Mecklenburg Library, May 12, 2021, www.cmlibrary.org/blog/fallacy-strong-black-woman.

[2] Rhonda Wells-Wilbon and Gaynell Marie Simpson, "Transitioning the Caregiving Role for the Next Generation: An African-Centered Womanist Perspective," *Black Women, Gender + Families 3*, no. 2 (Fall 2009): 87-105.

[3] Nilwona Nowlin, "Caregiving for Aging Parents and Family Members," Evangelical Covenant Church, https://covchurch.org/wp-content/uploads/2022/12/Crescendo -Caring-For-Aging-Parents-and-Family-Members-Guide-DIGITAL.pdf.

[4] Brianne L. Overton and R. Rocco Cottone, "Anticipatory Grief: A Family Systems Approach," *The Family Journal* 24, no. 4 (2016): 430-42, https://doi.org/10.1177/1066480716663490.

[5] *Merriam-Webster.com Dictionary*, s.v. "strong," accessed July 19, 2024, www.merriam-webster.com/dictionary/strong.

[6] Kelly Yu-Hsin Liao, Meifen Wei, and Mengxi Yin, "The Misunderstood Schema of the Strong Black Woman: Exploring Its Mental Health Consequences and Coping Responses Among African American Women," *Psychology of Women Quarterly* 44, no. 1 (2019): 84-104.

[7] Liao, Wei, and Yin, "The Misunderstood Schema," 84-104.

[8] *Oxford Languages*, (Oxford University Press), s.v. "dust," www.google.com/search?q=dust+definition&oq=dust&aqs.

[9] *Dictionary.com*, s.v. "what doesn't kill you makes you stronger," www.dictionary.com/e/slang/what-doesnt-kill-you-makes-you-stronger/.

2. WORTHY OF LOVE

[1] Sasha Santhakumar, "What to Know about Melanin," *Medical News Today*, Healthline Media, April 29, 2021, www.medicalnewstoday.com/articles/melanin.

[2] Asha DuMonthier, Chandra Childers, and Jessica Milli, "The Status of Black Women in the United States," Institute for Women's Policy Research, iwpr.org/wp-content/uploads/2020/08/SOBW_ExecutiveSummary_Digital-2.pdf.

[3] Katie Lange, "All Black Female WWII Unit to Receive Congressional Gold Medal," *DOD News*, US Department of Defense, March 18, 2022, www.defense.gov/News/Feature-Stories/story/Article/2971608/all-black-female-wwii-unit-to-receive-congressional-gold-medal/.

[4] Natasha Smith, "When We Met Jesus," *Prodigal*, HopeFront Music, 2023.

3. REPRESENTATION MATTERS

[1] Erica Richards, "The State of Mental Health of Black Women: Clinical Considerations," *Psychiatric Times* 38, no. 9, September 23, 2021.

[2] Dimitrije Curcic, "Black Authors Statistics," WordsRated, May 12, 2023, www.wordsrated.com/black-authors-statistics/.

[3] Natasha Sistrunk Robinson, *A Sojourner's Truth: Choosing Freedom and Courage in a Divided World* (Downers Grove, IL: InterVarsity Press, 2018), 53.

[4] Peter Scazzero, *Emotionally Healthy Spirituality (Updated Edition): It's Impossible to be Spiritually Mature While Remaining Emotionally Immature* (Grand Rapids, MI: Zondervan, 2017), 56-57.

[5] Scazzero, *Emotionally Healthy Spirituality*, 62-68.

[6] Scazzero, *Emotionally Healthy Spirituality*, 62-68.

4. ENOUGH IS ENOUGH

[1] Khushbu Shah and Juweek Adolphe. "400 Years Since Slavery: A Timeline of American History," *The Guardian*, August 16, 2019, www.theguardian.com /news/2019/aug/15/400-years-since-slavery-timeline.

[2] Paula A. Braveman et al., "Systemic and Structural Racism: Definitions, Examples, Health Damages, and Approaches to Dismantling," *Health Affairs* 41, no. 2 (2022): 171-78.

[3] Monnica T. Williams, "Colorblind Ideology Is a Form of Racism," *Psychology Today*, December 27, 2011, www.psychologytoday.com/us/blog/culturally-speaking/201112 /colorblind-ideology-is-form-racism.

[4] "Modern Day Abolition," National Underground Railroad Freedom Center, www .freedomcenter.org/learn/modern-day-abolition/.

[5] David K. Fremon, *The Jim Crow Laws and Racism in United States History* (New York: Enslow Publishing, 2014).

[6] "Racial Injustice and Broken Systems," Chalmers, August 11, 2020, www.chalmers .org/resources/blog/racial-injustice-and-broken-systems/.

[7] Earlise C. Ward and Susan M. Heidrich, "African American Women's Beliefs about Mental Illness, Stigma, and Preferred Coping Behaviors," *Research in Nursing and Health* 32, no. 5 (2009): 480-92.

[8] Ward and Heidrich, "African American Women's Beliefs," 480-92.

[9] Jamila K. Taylor, "Structural Racism and Maternal Health Among Black Women," *The Journal of Law, Medicine & Ethics* 48, no. 3 (2020): 506-17.

[10] Taylor, "Structural Racism and Maternal Health among Black Women," 506-17.

[11] Taylor, "Structural Racism and Maternal Health among Black Women," 506-17.

[12] Taylor, "Structural Racism and Maternal Health among Black Women," 506-17.

[13] Paula A. Braveman, Elaine Arkin, Dwayne Proctor, Tina Kauh, and Nicole Holm, "Systemic and Structural Racism: Definitions, Examples, Health Damages, and Approaches to Dismantling," Health Affairs 41, no. 2 (Feb 2022): 171-73, www .proquest.com/scholarly-journals/systemic-structural-racism-definitions-examples /docview/2627195062/se-2.

[14] "Slavery by Another Name," *PBS*, February 12, 2012, video, www.pbs.org/video /slavery-another-name-slavery-video/.

[15] Henry H. Wu et al., "Say Their Names: Resurgence in the Collective Attention Toward Black Victims of Fatal Police Violence Following the Death of George Floyd," *PLoS One* 18, no. 1 (January 11, 2023).

5. COURAGEOUS FAITH

[1] Natasha Smith, "Sitting with the Reality of Suffering (Paul Borthwick)," October 2023, in *Can You Just Sit with Me? with Natasha Smith*, produced by Spotify, podcast,

49:34, www.spreaker.com/episode/sitting-with-the-reality-of-suffering-paul-borthwick --56876657.

[2] "Emmett Till's Funeral," PBS, video, www.pbs.org/wgbh/americanexperience/features /emmett-tills-funeral/.

[3] "Emmett Till's Funeral."

[4] Devery S. Anderson, *Emmett Till: The Murder That Shocked the World and Propelled the Civil Rights Movement* (Jackson: University Press of Mississippi, 2015).

[5] Anderson, *Emmett Till*, 128.

[6] Anderson, *Emmett Till*, xxx, prologue.

[7] Lois Tonkin, "Growing Around Grief—Another Way of Looking at Grief and Recovery," *Bereavement Care* 15, no. 1 (1996):10.

[8] Daniel Miller, "What Is Anticipatory Grief?," *Psychology Today,* March 1, 2022, www.psychologytoday.com/us/blog/end-life-matters/202203/what-is-anticipatory -grief.

[9] MasterClass, "Othering Definition: How to Combat Othering in Your Daily Life," MasterClass, November 13, 2022, www.masterclass.com/articles/othering.

[10] Sheila Wise Rowe, *Young, Gifted, and Black: A Journey of Lament and Celebration* (Downers Grove, IL: InterVarsity Press, 2022), 99.

[11] MasterClass, "Othering Definition."

[12] Amber Jean-Marie Pabon and Vincent Basile, "It Don't Affect Them Like It Affects Us: Disenfranchised Grief of Black Boys in the Wake of Peer Homicide," *The Urban Review* 54, no. 1 (March 2022): 67-82, www.researchgate.net/publication /351042749_It_Don't_Affect_Them_Like_it_Affects_Us_Disenfranchised_Grief _of_Black_Boys_in_the_Wake_of_Peer_Homicide.

[13] Robert A. Neimeyer and John R. Jordan, "Does Grief Counseling Work?," *Death Studies*, November 2003, 27(9):765-86, https://doi.org/10.1080/713842360.

[14] Charm Villalon, "8 Signs You Are Bitter: How to Stop It and Live a Happier Life," Inspiring Tips, May 2, 2022, www.inspiringtips.com/?s=signs+you+are+bitter.

[15] Mary-Frances O'Connor, *The Grieving Brain: The Surprising Science of How We Learn from Love and Loss* (New York: HarperOne, 2022), 160.

[16] *Cambridge Dictionary* (Cambridge University Press & Assessment), s.v. "Resistance," www.dictionary.cambridge.org/us/dictionary/english/resistance.

6. THIS IS FREEDOM

[1] *The Avengers*, directed by Joss Whedon (Burbank, CA: Walt Disney Studios, 2012).

[2] J. Celeste Walley-Jean, "Debunking the Myth of the 'Angry Black Woman': An Exploration of Anger in Young African American Women," *Black Women, Gender + Families* 3, no. 2 (2009): 68-86.

[3] Sanjana Gupta, "What to Know About the Anger Stage of Grief," Verywell Mind, December 4, 2023, www.verywellmind.com/the-anger-stage-of-grief-characteristics -and-coping-5295703.

[4] Sheila Wise Rowe, *Healing Racial Trauma: The Road to Resilience* (Downers Grove, IL: InterVarsity Press, 2020).

[5] Da'Mere T. Wilson and Mary Frances-O'Connor, "From Grief to Grievance: Combined Axes of Personal and Collective Grief Among Black Americans," *Frontiers in Psychiatry* 13, no. 850994 (2022).

[6] Edy Nathan, "5 Power Tools to Reset Grief's Anger," *Psychology Today*, August 22, 2022, www.psychologytoday.com/us/blog/tales-grief/202208/5-power-tools-reset -griefs-anger.

[7] C. S. Lewis, *A Grief Observed* (San Francisco: HarperSanFrancisco, 2001).

[8] Jacek Debiec and Joseph LeDoux, "Fear and the Brain," *Social Research* 71, no. 4 (Winter 2004): 807-18, www.proquest.com/scholarly-journals/fear-brain/docview /209672359/se-2.

[9] Martin R. Huecker et al., "Imposter Phenomenon," *StatPearls* (July 31, 2023), www .ncbi.nlm.nih.gov/books/NBK585058/.

[10] Huecker et al., "Imposter Phenomenon."

[11] Huecker et al., "Imposter Phenomenon."

[12] Gabriela Picciotto and Jesse Fox, "Exploring Experts' Perspectives on Spiritual Bypass: A Conventional Content Analysis," *Pastoral Psychology* 67, no. 1 (February 2018): 65-84, www.proquest.com/scholarly-journals/exploring-experts-perspectives -on-spiritual/docview/1977094061/se-2.

[13] Paul C. Rosenblatt and Beverly R. Wallace, *African American Grief* (Taylor & Francis Group, 2013).

[14] Rowe, *Healing Racial Trauma*, 56.

7. UNHINGED HEALING

[1] *APA Dictionary of Psychology* (American Psychological Association), s.v. "Trauma," https://dictionary.apa.org/trauma.

[2] Tihamer Bakó and Katalin Zana, *Transgenerational Trauma and Therapy: The Transgenerational Atmosphere* (London: Routledge, 2020), www.taylorfrancis .com/books/mono/10.4324/9781003015840/transgenerational-trauma-therapy-tiham %C3%A9r-bak%C3%B3-katalin-zana.

[3] Bessel van der Kolk, *The Body Keeps the Score: Brain, Mind, and Body in the Healing of Trauma* (New York: Penguin Books, 2014), 86.

[4] "Signs of Emotional Trauma in Adults," Fort Behavioral Health, December 29, 2022, www.fortbehavioral.com/addiction-recovery-blog/signs-of-emotional-trauma-in-adults/.

5 Van der Kolk, *The Body Keeps the Score*, 205.

6 Van der Kolk, *The Body Keeps the Score*, 205-6.

7 E. J. Jenkins, "Black Women and Community Violence: Trauma, Grief, and Coping," *Women & Therapy*, 2002, 25(3-4), 29-44, https://doi.org/10.1300/J015v25n03_03.

8 Van der Kolk, *The Body Keeps the Score*, 21.

9 Sheila Wise Rowe, *Healing Racial Trauma: The Road to Resilience* (Downers Grove, IL: InterVarsity Press, 2020): 10-15.

10 Nikki M. Taylor, *Driven Toward Madness: The Fugitive Slave Margaret Garner and Tragedy on the Ohio* (Athens: Ohio University Press, 2016).

11 Carol Fredrek, "3 Stages of Recovery from Trauma & PTSD in Therapy," Healing Matters, https://healingmatters.ca/3-stages-of-recovery-from-trauma-ptsd -in-therapy/.

12 Tihamér Bakó and Katalin Zana, *Transgenerational Trauma and Therapy: The Transgenerational Atmosphere* (New York: Routledge, 2020).

13 Bakó and Zana, *Transgenerational Trauma*, 20.

8. REST AS RESISTANCE

1 Eboni T. Herbert Harris et al., "Rest Among African American Women," *Holistic Nursing Practice* 32, no. 3 (2018): 143-48, https://doi.org/10.1097/HNP.0000000000000262.

2 Diane C. Lim et al., "The Need to Promote Sleep Health in Public Health Agendas Across the Globe," *Lancet Public Health* 8, no. 10 (2023): www.thelancet.com /journals/lanpub/article/PIIS2468-2667(23)00182-2/fulltext.

3 Solomon Ayalew, "The Power of Rest: Examining the Racial Disparities of Sleep and Its Connections to Black Health Outcomes," *Congressional Black Caucus Foundation* (2023), https://issuu.com/congressionalblackcaucusfoundation/docs /cbcf_nrei_sleep_research.

4 Saundra Dalton-Smith, *Sacred Rest: Recover Your Life, Renew Your Energy, Restore Your Sanity* (FaithWords, 2017).

5 Peter Scazzero, *Emotionally Healthy Spirituality* (Grand Rapids, MI: Zondervan, 2017).

6 R. A. Swenson, *Margin: Restoring Emotional, Physical, Financial, and Time Reserves to Overloaded Lives* (Colorado Springs, CO: NavPress, 2004), 56.

9. THE SOFTER LIFE

1 "Women in the Workplace," McKinsey & Company, 2023, https://womeninthework place.com.

2 *Dictionary.com* (Dictionary.com, LLC), s.v. "Stress," www.dictionary.com/browse/stress.

3 Meghan Tipre and Tiffany L. Carson, "A Qualitative Assessment of Gender- and Race-Related Stress Among Black Women," Womens Health Rep (New Rochelle) 3, no. 1 (2022): 222-27, https://doi.org/10.1089/whr.2021.0041.

[4] Alexander J. Hish et al., "Applying the Stress Process Model to Stress-Burnout and Stress-Depression Relationships in Biomedical Doctoral Students: A Cross-Sectional Pilot Study," *CBE Life Sciences Education* 18, no. 4 (2019): ar51, https://doi.org/10.1187/cbe.19-03-0060.

[5] Philip A. Rozario and Daniel DeRienzis, "Familism Beliefs and Psychological Distress Among African American Women Caregivers," *The Gerontologist* 48, no. 6 (2008): 772-80, https://doi.org/10.1093/geront/48.6.772.

[6] Bonnie T. Blankenship, "The Stress Process in Physical Education," *Journal of Physical Education, Recreation & Dance* 78, no. 6 (2007): 39-44, https://eric.ed.gov/?id=EJ795578#.

[7] Stacy Jackson, "Black Women are Unapologetically Tapping into their 'Soft Life' Energy in 2023," *Black Enterprise*, January 4, 2023, www.blackenterprise.com/black-women-are-unapologetically-tapping-into-their-soft-life-energy-in-2023/.

[8] Jennimai Nguyen, "Black Women Started Living the Soft Life. Then Came Quiet Quitting," *Mashable,* October 6, 2022, https://mashable.com/article/soft-life-quiet-quitting-trend.

[9] Jodi Grubbs, *Live Slowly: A Gentle Invitation to Exhale* (Downers Grove, IL: InterVarsity Press, 2024), 5.

[10] "The Kingdom of God: Already Here, But Not Yet Fully," Dr. Jim's Essential Bible Teaching, June 23, 2023, https://drjimsebt.com/2023/06/23/5-the-kingdom-of-god-already-here-but-not-yet-fully/.

[11] Bessel van der Kolk, M.D., *The Body Keeps the Score: Brain, Mind, and Body in the Healing of Trauma* (New York: Penguin Books, 2014), 27.

10. HOPE MATTERS

[1] Eileen Guenther, "In Their Own Words: Slave Life and the Power of Spirituals," *Musforum,* November 2016, https://musforum.org/in-their-own-words-slave-life-and-the-power-of-spirituals-by-eileen-guenther/#.

[2] Harriet Jacobs, *Incidents in the Life of a Slave Girl* (New York: G&D Media, 2020), 13.

[3] Camille Preston, "The Psychology of Hope," *Psychology Today*, October 24, 2021, www.psychologytoday.com/us/blog/mental-health-in-the-workplace/202110/the-psychology-of-hope.

[4] C. R. Snyder, *The Psychology of Hope: You Can Get There from Here* (New York: Free Press, 1994).

11. FAITH MARCHES ON

[1] Clare Bidwell Smith, *Conscious Grieving: A Transformative Approach to Healing from Loss* (New York: Workman Publishing, 2024), 38.

[2] Cole Arthur Riley, *Black Liturgies: Prayers, Poems, and Meditations for Staying Human* (New York: Convergent Books, 2024), 90.

[3] Peter Scazzero, *Emotionally Healthy Spirituality* (Grand Rapids, MI: Zondervan, 2024, 2017).

12. HEALING AND WHOLENESS

[1] "Mary Church Terrell's Advocacy & Impact on Voting Rights," NowThis, November 4, 2022, video, https://youtu.be/BtXx27RJS1I?si=zCQKICxKd7v2zTdT.

[2] Paris B. Adkins-Jackson, Portia A. Jackson Preston, and Teah Hairston, "'The Only Way Out': How Self-Care Is Conceptualized by Black Women," *Ethnicity & Health* 28, no. 1 (2023): 29-45.

[3] Adkins-Jackson et al., "'The Only Way Out,'" 29-45.

[4] Barbara L. Peacock, *Soul Care in African American Practice* (Downers Grove, IL: InterVarsity Press, 2020).

[5] Terra McDaniel, *Hopeful Lament: Tending Our Grief Through Spiritual Practices* (Downers Grove, IL: InterVarsity Press, 2023), 34, 65.

[6] *Dictionary.com* (Dictionary.com, LLC), s.v. "Black Girl Magic," www.dictionary.com/e/slang/black-girl-magic/.

[7] "Martin Luther King, Jr. Memorial: Quotations," National Park Service, www.nps.gov/mlkm/learn/quotations.htm.

[8] Madeleine L'Engle, *Two-Part Invention : The Story of a Marriage* (New York: Open Road Integrated Media, 2020), ebook, 76.

ALSO BY NATASHA SMITH

Can You Just Sit with Me?
978-1-5140-0621-4

Like this book?
Scan the code to discover more content like this!

Get on IVP's
email list to
receive special
offers, exclusive
book news,
and thoughtful
content from
your favorite authors on
topics you care about.

 InterVarsity Press

IVPRESS.COM/BOOK-QR